THE SECOND GRADE
BIG GET READY
BOOK

AUTHORS
ARLENE HENKEL
BARBARA GREGORICH
JEAN SYSWERDA
SHIRLEY LANE
ROBERTA BANNISTER

ILLUSTRATORS
CHRIS COOK
ROBIN KOONTZ
JOE BODDY

The Second Grade **Big Get Ready** Book is a compilation of favorite titles from the **Lift Off!** and **I Know It!** series. The ten titles are listed in the table of contents.

CONTENTS

	PAGES
READING SENTENCES	3–32
READING STORIES	33–64
MATH	65–96
SPELLING PUZZLES	97–128
BLENDS	129–160
PHONICS REVIEW	161–192
WORD SKILLS	193–224
SPELLING	225–256
LANGUAGE SKILLS	257–288
ADDITION & SUBTRACTION	289–320

An answer key is provided at the end of each skill area.

PARENT GUIDE

The skills in the **Big Get Ready Book** for Second Grade are those most commonly taught at the second grade level. Here are some suggestions for working with your child at home:

- Don't do too many pages at one sitting. The size of the book could overwhelm the child. Remove a few pages at a time. (Pages are perforated for easy removal.) Praise each completed page. Page by page, day to day, is the best.

- If your child is puzzled by one activity, move on to another. The activities are ordered, but there's nothing magical about that order.

- Do the activities at a particular time of day, perhaps before snack time. Do them when the child is not tired. Discuss the learning experience, be enthusiastic. "Let's work in our school books today! Do you remember what you did yesterday?"

- Enjoy it! Laugh a lot! Discuss the activity. Most activities can be done independently by the child since directions are clear and consistent. Never use an activity as punishment. Don't expect too much. The activities are meant as practice.

- There will be days when your child may not feel like working. This is typical, so accept it. And remember: the communication patterns you establish today will pay off as your child grows older.

Circle the sentence that goes with each picture.

Brave Bear counts the eggs.
Brave Bear carries the eggs.

The goat saw a truck.
The goat saw the turtle.

The elephant eats peanuts.
The elephant sells peanuts.

FOR SALE

The rabbit wins the race
Both rabbits win the race.

FINISH LINE

I keep pennies in a jar.
I keep eggs in a basket.

The dragon ate the dish.
The dragon held a candle.

My pocket is in my shoe.
My shoe is in my pocket.

Circle the sentence that goes with each picture.

Dad is high up on the ladder.
Dad is low on the ladder.

Wow! What a big cupcake!
Wow! What a big chicken!

Two lamps moved the lion.
Two lambs moved the lion.

Feathers fell on Brave Bear.
Brave Bear fell on the feathers.

The fence jumped over the horse.
The horse jumped over the fence.

The cat drank milk from a bowl.
Across the street walked the cat.

Brave Bear looks for honey.
Brave Bear hunts for his horn.

4

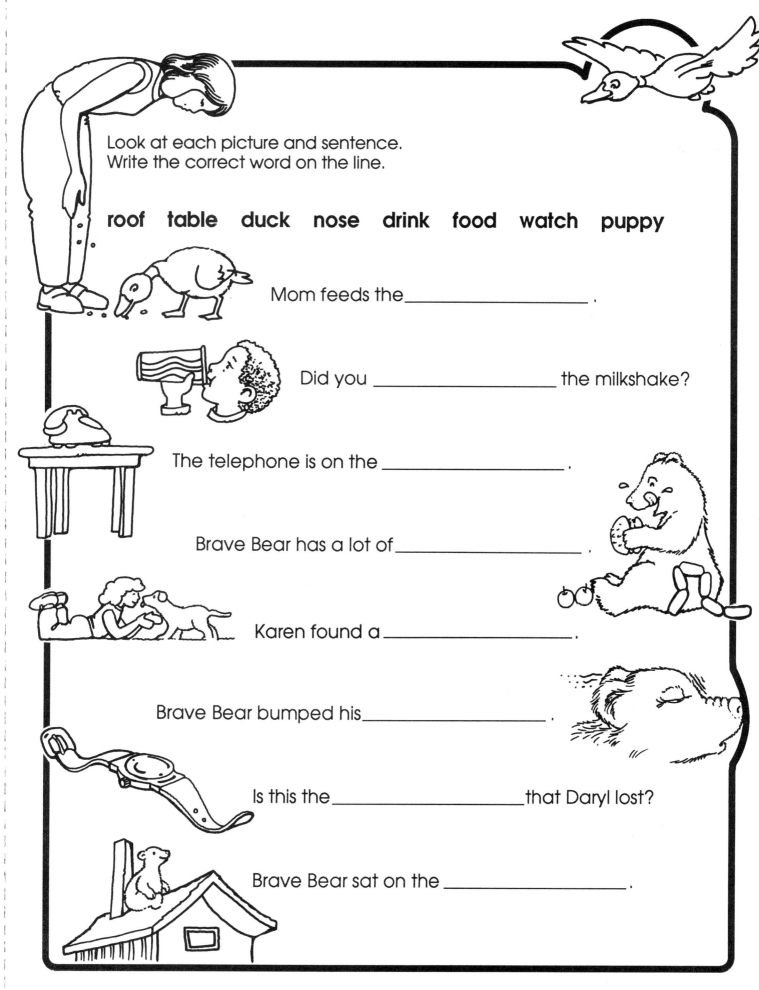

Look at each picture and sentence.
Write the correct word on the line.

roof   table   duck   nose   drink   food   watch   puppy

Mom feeds the _____ .

Did you _____ the milkshake?

The telephone is on the _____ .

Brave Bear has a lot of _____ .

Karen found a _____ .

Brave Bear bumped his _____ .

Is this the _____ that Daryl lost?

Brave Bear sat on the _____ .

Look at each picture and sentence.
Write the correct word on the line.

glove   bird   climb   school   prize   blew   kitten   plant

The_____ was in the basket.

Jed took his monkey to _____ .

I won first _____ .

Whose_____ is this?

Alan likes to _____ flowers.

Mr. James _____ the whistle.

Will the clown_____that pole?

Brave Bear likes the _____ .

6

Read each sentence.
Do what it says.

Draw a **circle** around Brave Bear.

Color the larger shirt **red**.

Color the other shirt **yellow**.

Draw a **box** around the telephone.

Write **L** on the left skate.

Write **R** on the right skate.

Count the whistles.

There are _____ of them.

Read each sentence.
Do what it says.

Draw a **line** from Brave Bear to the picture of the breakfast.

Write an **X** on the picture of the lunch.

Draw a **circle** around the smaller man.

Draw a **box** around the other man.

Write **A** on the picture of the apple pie.

Write **C** on the picture of the cherry pie.

Draw a **pie** and divide it into **four** pieces.

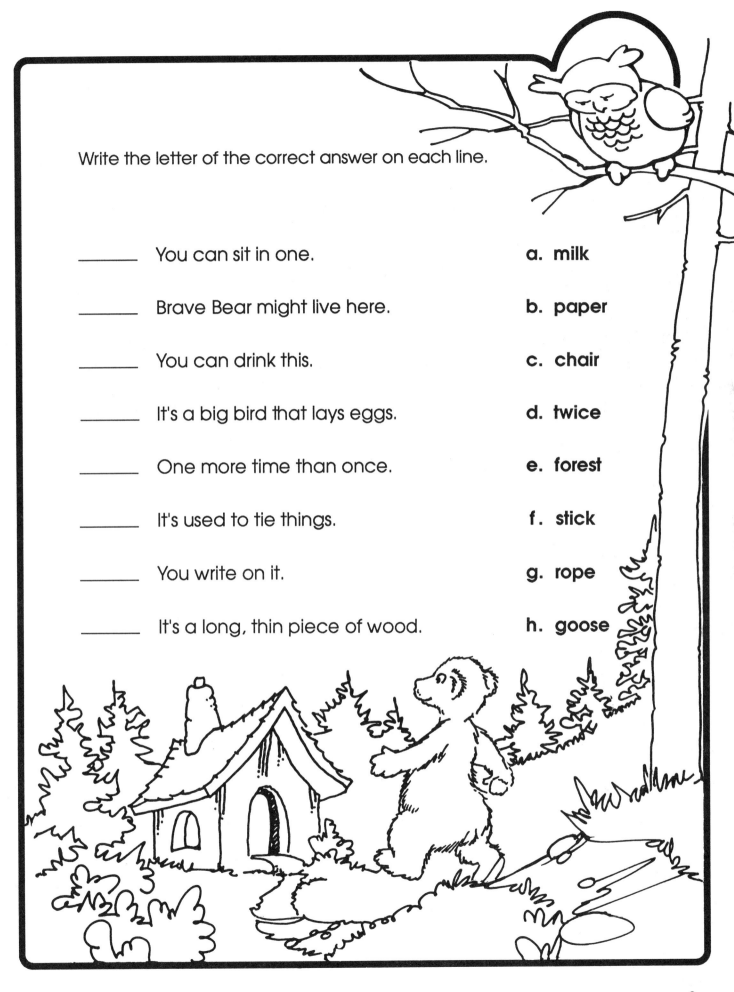

Write the letter of the correct answer on each line.

_____ You can sit in one.   **a. milk**

_____ Brave Bear might live here.   **b. paper**

_____ You can drink this.   **c. chair**

_____ It's a big bird that lays eggs.   **d. twice**

_____ One more time than once.   **e. forest**

_____ It's used to tie things.   **f. stick**

_____ You write on it.   **g. rope**

_____ It's a long, thin piece of wood. **h. goose**

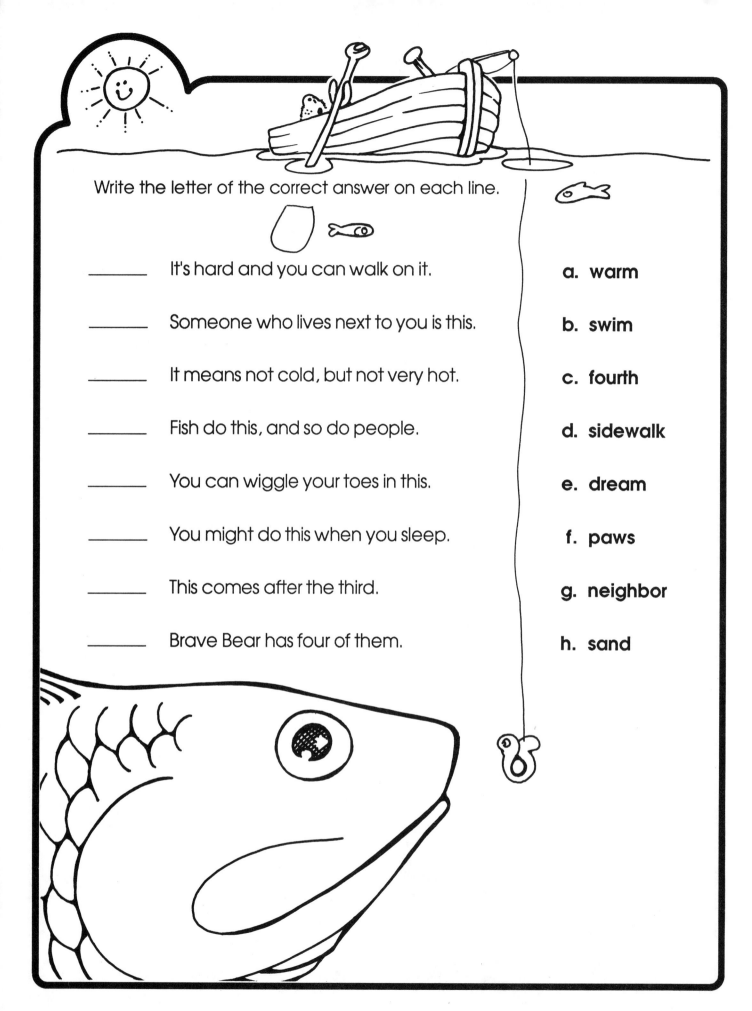

Write the letter of the correct answer on each line.

_____ It's hard and you can walk on it.

_____ Someone who lives next to you is this.

_____ It means not cold, but not very hot.

_____ Fish do this, and so do people.

_____ You can wiggle your toes in this.

_____ You might do this when you sleep.

_____ This comes after the third.

_____ Brave Bear has four of them.

a. warm

b. swim

c. fourth

d. sidewalk

e. dream

f. paws

g. neighbor

h. sand

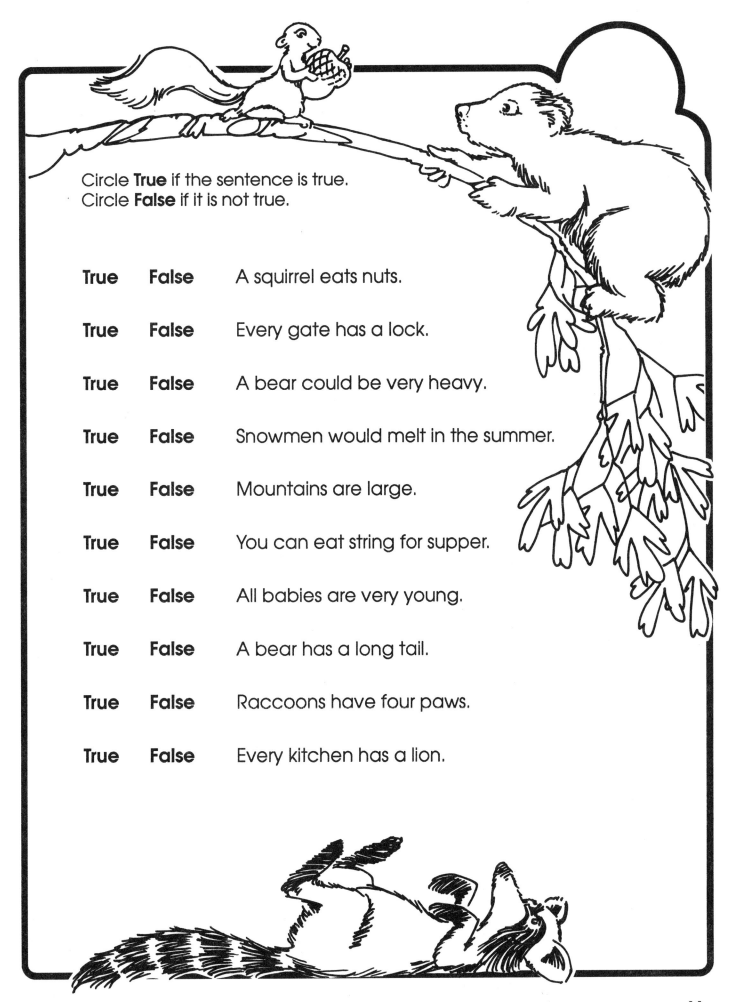

Circle **True** if the sentence is true.
Circle **False** if it is not true.

True　　**False**　　A squirrel eats nuts.

True　　**False**　　Every gate has a lock.

True　　**False**　　A bear could be very heavy.

True　　**False**　　Snowmen would melt in the summer.

True　　**False**　　Mountains are large.

True　　**False**　　You can eat string for supper.

True　　**False**　　All babies are very young.

True　　**False**　　A bear has a long tail.

True　　**False**　　Raccoons have four paws.

True　　**False**　　Every kitchen has a lion.

Circle **True** if the sentence is true.
Circle **False** if it is not true.

True	**False**	A face has two eyes, one nose, and two mouths.
True	**False**	You can cut a pie into pieces.
True	**False**	A robin is a fish.
True	**False**	There are two wheels on a bike.
True	**False**	A bear might drink water from a stream.
True	**False**	Some people live in apartments.
True	**False**	You can keep cake in a bottle.
True	**False**	A sad person is very happy.
True	**False**	Cows live in a barn or in a field.
True	**False**	You can bake food in an oven.

12

Words that rhyme have the same last sound.
Who, zoo, blue, and **you** all rhyme.

Read each sentence at the top of the page.
Write it below the sentence it rhymes with
at the bottom of the page.

Brave Bear shakes the **floor**.

Brave Bear is very **cold**.

He will hide behind the **chair**.

Down the hill he will **go**.

Brave Bear likes to **snore**.

Brave Bear shakes the floor.
_____

Brave Bear likes the **snow**.

_____

Brave Bear looks for **gold**.

_____

Brave Bear doesn't **care**.

_____

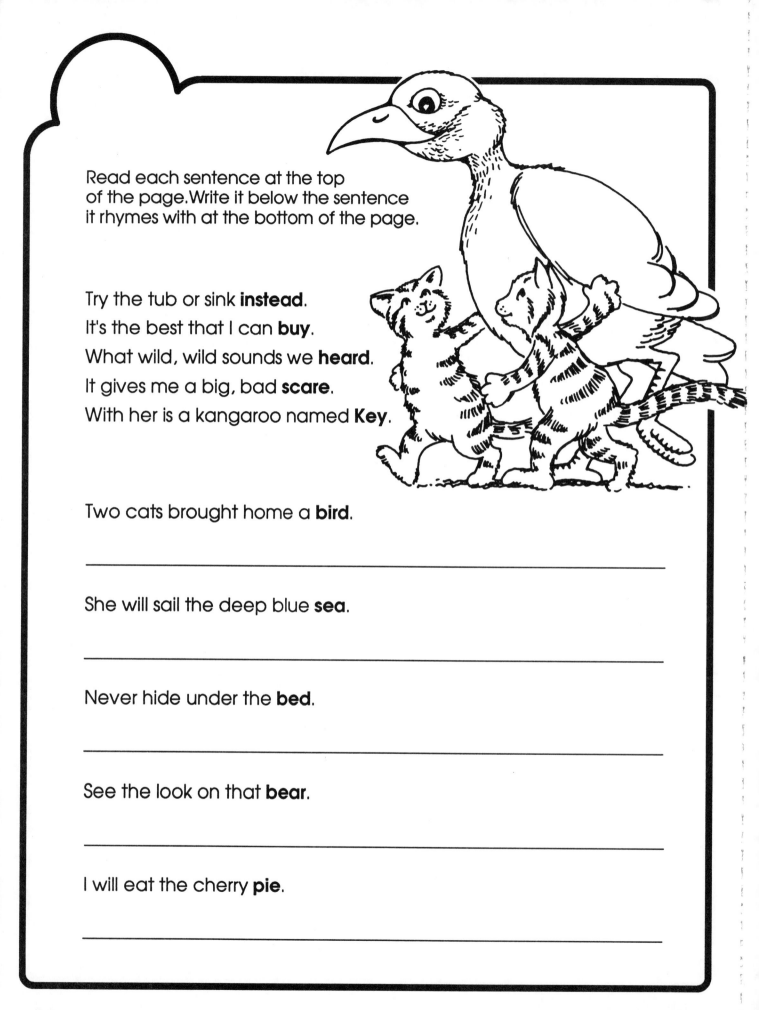

Read each sentence at the top of the page. Write it below the sentence it rhymes with at the bottom of the page.

Try the tub or sink **instead**.

It's the best that I can **buy**.

What wild, wild sounds we **heard**.

It gives me a big, bad **scare**.

With her is a kangaroo named **Key**.

Two cats brought home a **bird**.

_____

She will sail the deep blue **sea**.

_____

Never hide under the **bed**.

_____

See the look on that **bear**.

_____

I will eat the cherry **pie**.

_____

Look at each picture.
Read the question.
Write an **X** next to the sentence that tells the reason why.

Why is Emma happy?

_____ She does not like Yup, her dog.

_____ She must go to school.

_____ She likes her dog Yup, and Yup likes her.

Why is Brave Bear hot?

_____ It is winter.

_____ It is a hot summer day.

_____ He forgot his sunglasses.

Why is Dad tired?

_____ He is carrying heavy things.

_____ He does not like to go camping.

_____ The car is in the garage.

Why isn't Colin in school?

_____ He's going on a trip.

_____ He doesn't feel well.

_____ Today is his birthday.

Why is the dog sad?

_____ The dog does not like trees.

_____ The dog is very sleepy.

_____ The squirrel is dropping shells on it.

Look at each picture.
Read the question.
Write an **X** next to the sentence that tells the reason why.

Why is the parade late?

_____ The float is too big.

_____ A float has a flat tire.

_____ Too many people are in the street.

Why did the turtle win the race?

_____ Turtles run very fast.

_____ The rabbit let it win.

_____ The rabbit fell asleep.

Why are the skates broken?

_____ The elephant was too heavy for them.

_____ The skates were always broken.

_____ The elephant threw them away.

Why is Brave Bear wet?

_____ The rain is falling.

_____ Brave Bear is taking a bath.

_____ Brave Bear is taking a shower.

Why does the cowgirl have a rope?

_____ She wants to jump rope.

_____ She wants to catch the horse.

_____ She wants to fix the fence.

Look at each picture.
Read the question.
Write an **X** next to the sentence that tells the reason why.

Why is Max hurt?

_____ He fell on a bear.

_____ He fell off his bike.

_____ He should have walked home.

Why are the dishes dirty?

_____ The animals buy dirty dishes.

_____ The animals just finished dinner.

_____ The animals sell dirty dishes.

Why is Rosa afraid?

_____ She thinks she lost her dress.

_____ The closet is full of coats and shoes.

_____ She thinks a monster is in the closet.

Why does the woman scold Brave Bear?

_____ He ate the apples.

_____ He ate the pies.

_____ She doesn't like bears.

Why is the elevator empty?

_____ The elephants are afraid of the mouse.

_____ The mouse is afraid of the elephants.

_____ The elephants like peanuts.

Look at each picture.
Put an **X** next to the sentences that go with each picture.

____ The kangaroo is happy.

____ A plane is in the air.

____ The bowl is almost empty.

____ The glass is full.

____ The kangaroo is outside.

____ A monkey watches.

____ The bowl is very full.

____ The kangaroo is sad.

____ Two girls walk in the park.

____ A woman sits on a bench.

____ There are flowers in the park.

____ The boy walks his dog.

____ The woman sits outside.

____ The boy pulls a wagon.

____ A man feeds a squirrel.

____ It is a very cold day.

Look at each picture.
Put an **X** next to the sentences that go with each picture.

____ **Mom talks on the telephone.**

____ **It is early in the morning.**

____ **It is night time.**

____ **A toy dog is walking.**

____ **The baby eats ice cream.**

____ **The oven door is open.**

____ **The baby eats a cookie.**

____ **Dad and Emma help make dinner.**

____ **Brave Bear carries wood.**

____ **The rabbit laughs.**

____ **The fox sees birds.**

____ **The rabbit is not happy.**

____ **Brave Bear has a basket.**

____ **The squirrel holds the eggs.**

____ **A crow chases Brave Bear.**

____ **The raccoon holds a broom.**

Look at each picture.
Put an **X** next to the sentences that go with each picture.

____ The tower is quite tall.

____ In the tower is a princess.

____ The horse has no rider.

____ The princess has long hair.

____ Grass grows around the tower.

____ The rider is very old.

____ The rider sees the princess.

____ There are no windows
in the tower.

____ All the cars have stopped.

____ Three cars have stopped.

____ Brave Bear drives a car.

____ The policeman has a whistle.

____ The policeman is a woman.

____ Brave Bear holds a box.

____ A truck carries chickens.

____ People are crying.

Read each sentence.
Write the correct word on each line.

quiet	hole
tie	listen
pat	empty
send	city
lazy	early

"Please be _____ . Stop making that noise!"

I think the teacher is going to _____ us home.

"Six o'clock in the morning is very _____ ," growled Brave Bear.

_____ ! Do you hear the phone ringing?

I saw the rabbit run into its _____ .

Hold your finger here while I _____ the string.

Oh, oh! The lion's cage is _____ .

If I don't work hard, will you call me _____ ?

"Never _____ a bear on the head," growled Brave Bear.

A farmer does not work in the _____ .

Read each sentence.
Write the correct word on each line.

wing	**people**
shape	**friendly**
point	**win**
flew	**library**
finish	**splash**

Did the painter _____ painting this room?

Women, men, girls, and boys are _____ .

It is bad manners to _____ your finger at somebody.

Brave Bear returned the books to the _____ .

The robin _____ into the window.

A circle is a _____ . So is a square. So is a triangle.

Do you like to _____ in the swimming pool?

Who will _____ the race?

"Oh, oh," thought Jack. "I hope this giant is _____ ."

I have one more _____ to build on my model plane.

Read each sentence.
Write the correct word on each line.

doctor	branch
drive	tractor
sign	magic
few	bump
clever	remember

Sara's mother will _____ us to school.

The truck went over the _____ in the road.

The _____ gave me a shot.

Mr. Jackson could not _____ my name.

Brave Bear made a _____ that said STAY OUT!

Somebody who is very smart is _____ .

"I want to be a farmer and drive a _____ ," said Dawn.

This big _____ fell off that tree.

"We have only a _____ jars of honey left," said the man.

"It's _____ ," I said as I pulled a rabbit out of my hat.

Read each question.
Write an **X** next to the sentence that answers the question.

In what way are a boy, a flower, and a bear alike?

_____ They are all green.

_____ All are animals.

_____ All are alive.

In what way are a bridge, a sidewalk, and a floor alike?

_____ You can walk on each of them.

_____ All of them are soft and fluffy.

_____ They are always gray.

In what way are a dollar, a penny, and a dime alike?

_____ They are all made out of silver.

_____ All are square.

_____ They are all money.

In what way are a slide, a seesaw, and a chair alike?

_____ You can sit on each one.

_____ Each is a toy.

_____ You can find them in every house.

In what way are a farmer, a doctor, and a teacher alike?

_____ They are all men.

_____ They all work.

_____ All of them are women.

Read each question.
Write an **X** next to the sentence that answers the question.

In what way are a bell, a telephone, and a whistle alike?

_____ They can all make a sound.

_____ All are alive.

_____ You can blow each one.

In what way are a truck, a plane, and a boat alike?

_____ They all have two wings and four wheels.

_____ Every one is made of wood.

_____ Each will take you from one place to another place.

In what way are a notebook, a book, and a newspaper alike?

_____ None of them are paper.

_____ They are all made out of paper.

_____ None of them are white.

In what way are a bear, the dirt, and hair alike?

_____ They are all things to eat or drink.

_____ You have to brush each of them.

_____ Each one could be brown in color.

In what way are an aunt, an uncle, and a grandmother alike?

_____ Each of them is a woman.

_____ They all belong to a family.

_____ All of them go to work every day.

Read each question.
Write an **X** next to the sentence that answers the question.

In what way are a blueberry, corn, and a hamburger alike?

_____ They are all blue.

_____ All are plants.

_____ They are all food.

In what way are a bear, a deer, and a fox alike?

_____ They are always red in color.

_____ They all live in the woods.

_____ They all walk on two legs.

In what way are a basement, a bedroom, and a kitchen alike?

_____ They are cold and wet.

_____ They are parts of a house.

_____ They are all at the top of the stairs.

In what way are a shovel, a rake, and a hammer alike?

_____ Each is a tool.

_____ You can tie a box with each of them.

_____ They are always kept in the attic.

In what way are a monkey, a girl, and a raccoon alike?

_____ Each can hold things with its hands.

_____ They all wear gloves or mittens.

_____ All of them live in the deep, dark forest.

Read each riddle.
Write the correct answer on each line.

airport   swish

tower   bounce

gold   answer

lake   beehive

I am the tall, tall part
of a castle or house.

I'm a _____ .

I am where planes land
and many people wait.

I am called a _____ .

I am the way a ball comes up
when it hits the floor.

I'm a _____ .

A tail does this.
A broom does this.
What do they do?

They both go _____ .

I am the home to hundreds
who buzz in and out.

I am a _____ .

A pond is big, but I am bigger.
A rain is wet, but I am wetter.

I'm a _____ .

I am a color and I
am a lost treasure.

I am _____ .

I'm it! It is me!
I am what you're looking for
and what you need.

I am the _____ .

Read each riddle.
Write the correct answer on each line.

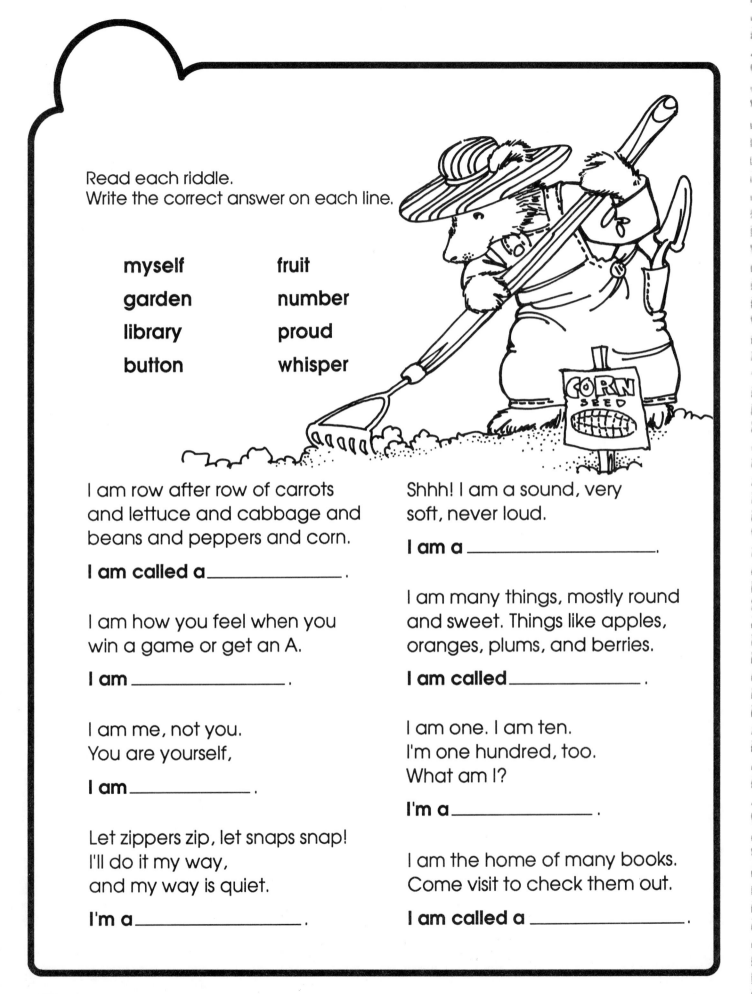

myself	fruit
garden	number
library	proud
button	whisper

I am row after row of carrots and lettuce and cabbage and beans and peppers and corn.

I am called a_____.

I am how you feel when you win a game or get an A.

I am _____.

I am me, not you.
You are yourself,

I am _____.

Let zippers zip, let snaps snap!
I'll do it my way,
and my way is quiet.

I'm a _____.

Shhh! I am a sound, very soft, never loud.

I am a _____.

I am many things, mostly round and sweet. Things like apples, oranges, plums, and berries.

I am called _____.

I am one. I am ten.
I'm one hundred, too.
What am I?

I'm a _____.

I am the home of many books.
Come visit to check them out.

I am called a _____.

Read each riddle.
Write the correct answer on each line.

iron   trouble

wrong   sand

above   pair

swan   yard

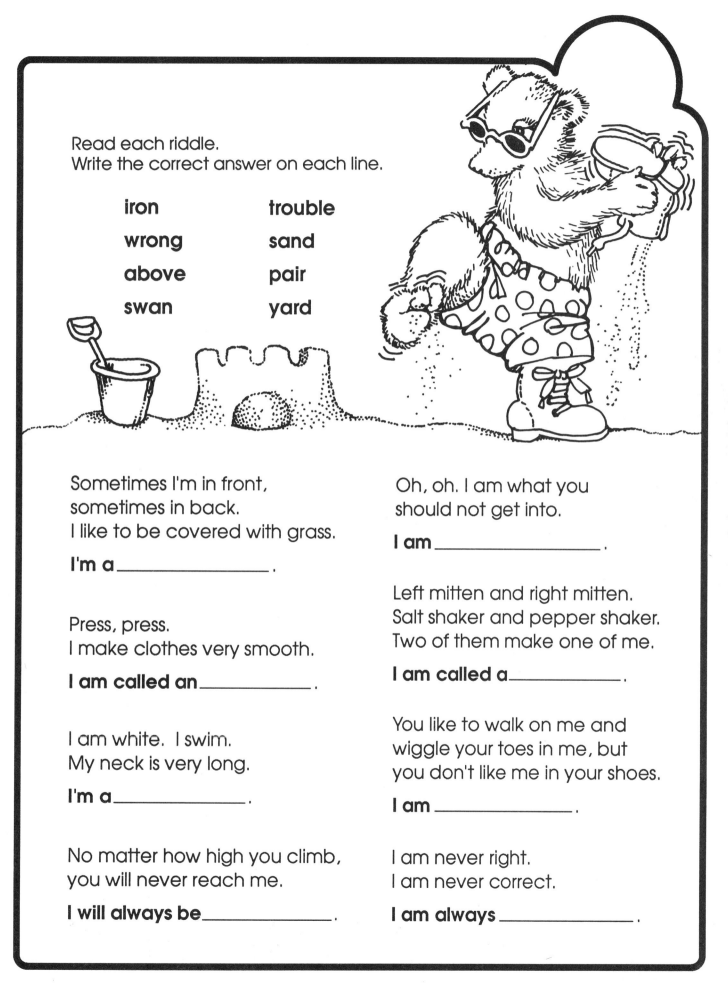

Sometimes I'm in front,
sometimes in back.
I like to be covered with grass.

I'm a_____ .

Press, press.
I make clothes very smooth.

I am called an_____ .

I am white. I swim.
My neck is very long.

I'm a_____ .

No matter how high you climb,
you will never reach me.

I will always be_____ .

Oh, oh. I am what you
should not get into.

I am_____ .

Left mitten and right mitten.
Salt shaker and pepper shaker.
Two of them make one of me.

I am called a_____ .

You like to walk on me and
wiggle your toes in me, but
you don't like me in your shoes.

I am_____ .

I am never right.
I am never correct.

I am always_____ .

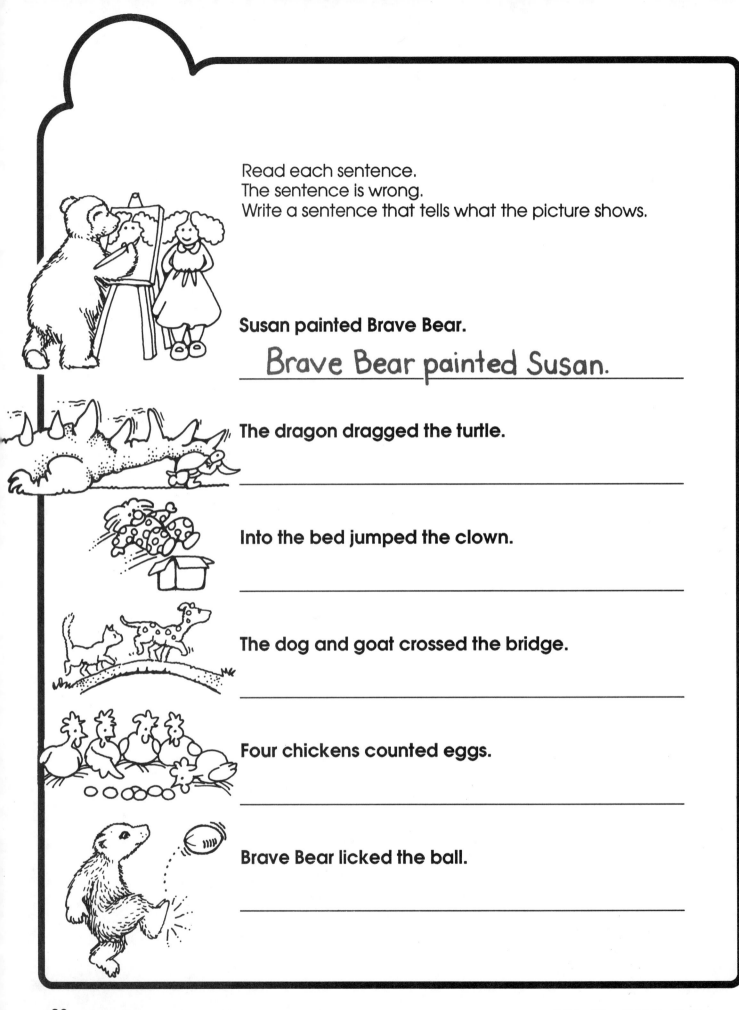

Read each sentence.
The sentence is wrong.
Write a sentence that tells what the picture shows.

Susan painted Brave Bear.

Brave Bear painted Susan.

The dragon dragged the turtle.

_____

Into the bed jumped the clown.

_____

The dog and goat crossed the bridge.

_____

Four chickens counted eggs.

_____

Brave Bear licked the ball.

_____

30

Page 3

Brave Bear counts the eggs.
The goat saw the turtle.
The elephant sells peanuts.
Both rabbits win the race.
I keep pennies in a jar.
The dragon held a candle.
My shoe is in my pocket.

Page 4

Dad is low on the ladder.
Wow! What a big cupcake!
Two lambs moved the lion.
Feathers fell on Brave Bear.
The horse jumped over the fence.
The cat drank milk from a bowl.
Brave Bear hunts for his horn.

Page 5

duck
drink
table
food
puppy
nose
watch
roof

Page 6	**Page 7**	**Page 9**	**Page 10**	**Page 11**	**Page 12**
kitten	6 (whistles)	c	d	True	False
school		e	g	False	True
prize		a	a	True	False
glove		h	b	True	True
plant		d	h	True	True
blew		g	e	False	True
climb		b	c	True	False
bird		f	f	False	False
				True	True
				False	True

Page 13

Brave Bear shakes the floor.
Down the hill he will go.
Brave Bear is very cold.
He will hide behind the chair.

Page 14

What wild, wild sounds we heard.
With her is a kangaroo named Key.
Try the tub or sink instead.
It gives me a big, bad scare.
It's the best that I can buy.

Page 15

She likes her dog Yup,
and Yup likes her.
It is a hot summer day.
He is carrying heavy things.
He doesn't feel well.
The squirrel is dropping
shells on it.

Page 16

A float has a flat tire.
The rabbit fell asleep.
The elephant was too
heavy for them.
Brave Bear is taking a shower.
She wants to catch the horse.

Page 17

He fell off his bike.
The animals just finished dinner.
She thinks a monster is in the closet.
He ate the apples.
The elephants are afraid
of the mouse.

Page 18

The kangaroo is happy.
The glass is full.
A monkey watches.
The bowl is very full.
A woman sits on a bench.
There are flowers in the park.
The boy walks his dog.
The woman sits outside.
A man feeds a squirrel.

Page 19

It is night time.
A toy dog is walking.
The oven door is open.
The baby eats a cookie.
Dad and Emma help make dinner.
Brave Bear carries wood.
The rabbit laughs.
The fox sees birds.
Brave Bear has a basket.
The raccoon holds a broom.

Page 20

The tower is quite tall.
In the tower is a princess.
The princess has long hair.
Grass grows around the tower.
The rider sees the princess.
Three cars have stopped.
The policeman has a whistle.
Brave Bear holds a box.
A truck carries chickens.

Page 21

quiet
send
early
Listen
hole
tie
empty
lazy
pat
city

Page 22

finish
people
point
library
flew
shape
splash
win
friendly
wing

Page 23

drive
bump
doctor
remember
sign
clever
tractor
branch
few
magic

Page 24

All are alive.
You can walk on
each of them.
They are all money.
You can sit on each one.
They all work.

Page 25

They can all make a sound.
Each will take you from one place
to another place.
They are all made out of paper.
Each one could be brown in color.
They all belong to a family.

Page 26

They are all food.
They all live in the woods.
They are parts of a house.
Each is a tool.
Each can hold things
with its hands.

Page 27

tower
airport
bounce
swish
beehive
lake
gold
answer

Page 28

garden
proud
myself
button
whisper
fruit
number
library

Page 29

yard
iron
swan
above
trouble
pair
sand
wrong

Page 30

Brave Bear painted Susan.
The turtle dragged the dragon.
Into the box jumped the clown.
The dog and cat crossed the
bridge.
Five chickens counted eggs.
Brave Bear kicked the ball.

What a House

Words that rhyme have the same last sound.
Do, **shoe**, and **blue** all rhyme.
Write in the missing words to finish the story.
Write in the word that rhymes with the **bold** word.

bed   house   honey   door   pet

One day a **mouse**

Moved into Brave Bear's ___house___ .

Brave Bear slept on the **floor.**

Right next to the _____ .

"Move right in," Brave Bear **said.**

"Find a place to put your _____."

"You'll find the bath is always **wet,**

Because I keep a whale as a _____."

"Things around here are always **funny.**

Take what you want, but don't take my _____."

Good Morning, Rabbit

Rabbit hears the clock. The clock is ringing. The sound wakes Rabbit up. He opens one eye. He looks at the clock. "Oh," says Rabbit. "Oh, no."

Then Rabbit rolls over. He still hears the clock ringing. So Rabbit sits up. He fold his big ears over. Now he cannot hear the clock. He goes back to sleep.

Somebody is shaking Rabbit – shaking him hard. He opens one eye. Oh, oh. It is Mother Rabbit. "Are you still sleeping?" She asks. "It is time to brush your teeth. It is time to eat breakfast. You are going to be late for school. Then I will not be happy."

Read each question below.
Write a sentence to answer each question.

Who is sleeping?

_____

What wakes Rabbit up?

_____

What does Rabbit fold over?

_____

Who shakes Rabbit?

_____

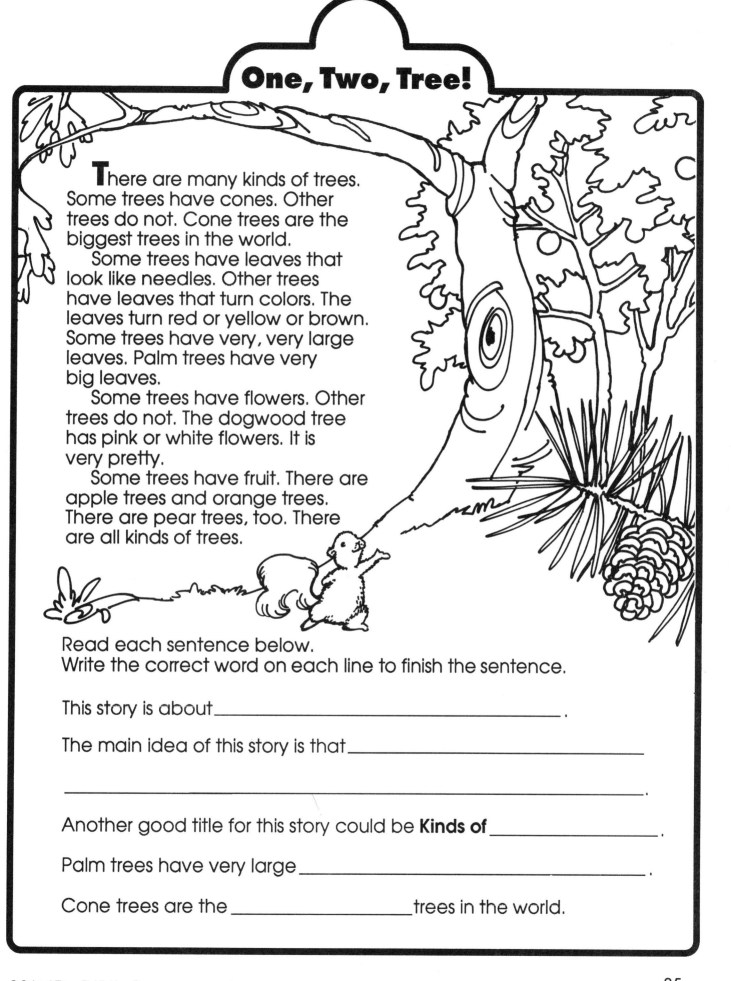

One, Two, Tree!

There are many kinds of trees. Some trees have cones. Other trees do not. Cone trees are the biggest trees in the world.

Some trees have leaves that look like needles. Other trees have leaves that turn colors. The leaves turn red or yellow or brown. Some trees have very, very large leaves. Palm trees have very big leaves.

Some trees have flowers. Other trees do not. The dogwood tree has pink or white flowers. It is very pretty.

Some trees have fruit. There are apple trees and orange trees. There are pear trees, too. There are all kinds of trees.

Read each sentence below.
Write the correct word on each line to finish the sentence.

This story is about_____.

The main idea of this story is that_____

_____.

Another good title for this story could be **Kinds of** _____.

Palm trees have very large _____.

Cone trees are the _____ trees in the world.

Brave Bear Digs

Brave Bear looked around his house. "I have a lot of honey," he said. "I need more space for my honey!" He thought a while. "I will dig a basement," he said. "Then I will have more space."

Brave Bear went into his bedroom. "This is where I will begin," he said. "I will dig straight down. Then I will have a basement."

"That is not correct," said Owl, who was there. "That is not correct."

But Brave Bear did not listen to Owl. No, Brave Bear dug. He dug in the bedroom. Soon he had a basement where his bedroom had been. Then he moved into another room. Brave Bear dug straight down through his whole house. "There," he said at last. "I have finished! I will keep my honey in the basement."

But when Brave Bear looked, all he saw was basement. "Where is my house?" shouted Brave Bear.

"It is in your basement," said Owl. "To dig a basement, you must dig under your house. You must not dig straight down through your house."

Read each question and circle the correct answer.

Where does Brave Bear begin to dig?
    basement   bedroom   hall

Does he dig straight down through the house?
    yes   no   never

Who says, "That is not correct"?
    Brave Bear   Owl   Honey

What does Brave Bear need more of?
    honey   space   basement

What does Brave Bear have a lot of?
    space   Owl   honey

The Dog and the Duck

Words that rhyme have the same last sound.
Do, shoe, and **blue** all rhyme.
Write in the missing words to finish the story.
Write in the word that rhymes with the **bold** word.

truck   **log**   **luck**   **bone**   **jog**

One day a duck and a **dog**

Sat in the woods on a _____ .

The dog said, "Here we are **alone**.

I don't even have a _____ ."

"We are lost," said the **duck**.

"What bad _____ ."

"I must go," said the **dog**.

"I can get home if I _____ ."

"Not me," said the **duck**.

"I always go home in a _____ ."

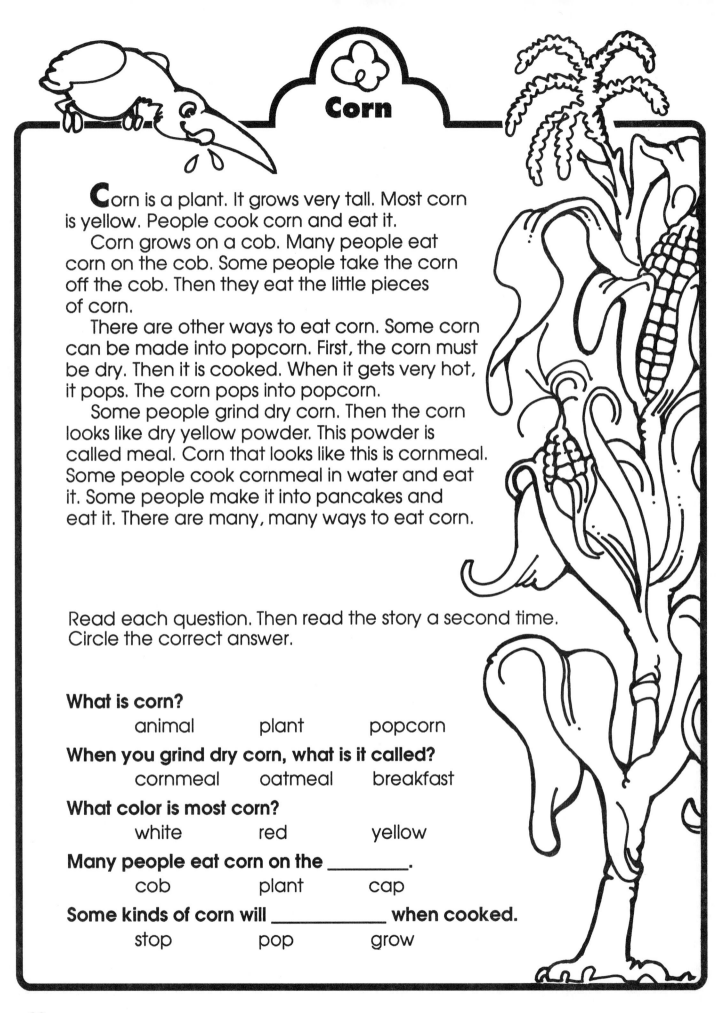

Corn

Corn is a plant. It grows very tall. Most corn is yellow. People cook corn and eat it.

Corn grows on a cob. Many people eat corn on the cob. Some people take the corn off the cob. Then they eat the little pieces of corn.

There are other ways to eat corn. Some corn can be made into popcorn. First, the corn must be dry. Then it is cooked. When it gets very hot, it pops. The corn pops into popcorn.

Some people grind dry corn. Then the corn looks like dry yellow powder. This powder is called meal. Corn that looks like this is cornmeal. Some people cook cornmeal in water and eat it. Some people make it into pancakes and eat it. There are many, many ways to eat corn.

Read each question. Then read the story a second time. Circle the correct answer.

What is corn?

animal   plant   popcorn

When you grind dry corn, what is it called?

cornmeal   oatmeal   breakfast

What color is most corn?

white   red   yellow

Many people eat corn on the _____.

cob   plant   cap

Some kinds of corn will _____ when cooked.

stop   pop   grow

Brave Bear Bakes

Too much honey! There was too much honey in Brave Bear's basement. "I know," said Brave Bear. "I will bake. I will bake things with honey. Then I will have less honey. So I will have more room."

"That might not be true," said Owl, who was watching.

"What do you know about honey?" asked Brave Bear. "You are an owl. Owls don't know about honey."

"I know about space," said Owl! "I know how things work."

But Brave Bear did not listen. Brave Bear baked. He baked honey cookies. Yum! He baked honey cakes and honey cupcakes. They were so good. He baked honey pancakes. He baked honey bread. It was good, too. He baked honey muffins.

When Brave Bear was done, he looked all around. "Help!" he shouted. "There is no room in my basement. There is even less room than there was before!"

"Baked things take up space," said Owl. "They take up more space than the honey you used to bake them."

What does each word mean?
Write the letter of the correct answer next to the word.

_____	**less**	**a.**	A sweet food made by bees
_____	**space**	**b.**	the lowest part of a house
_____	**honey**	**c.**	to cook in an oven
_____	**bake**	**d.**	room
_____	**basement**	**e.**	not as much as

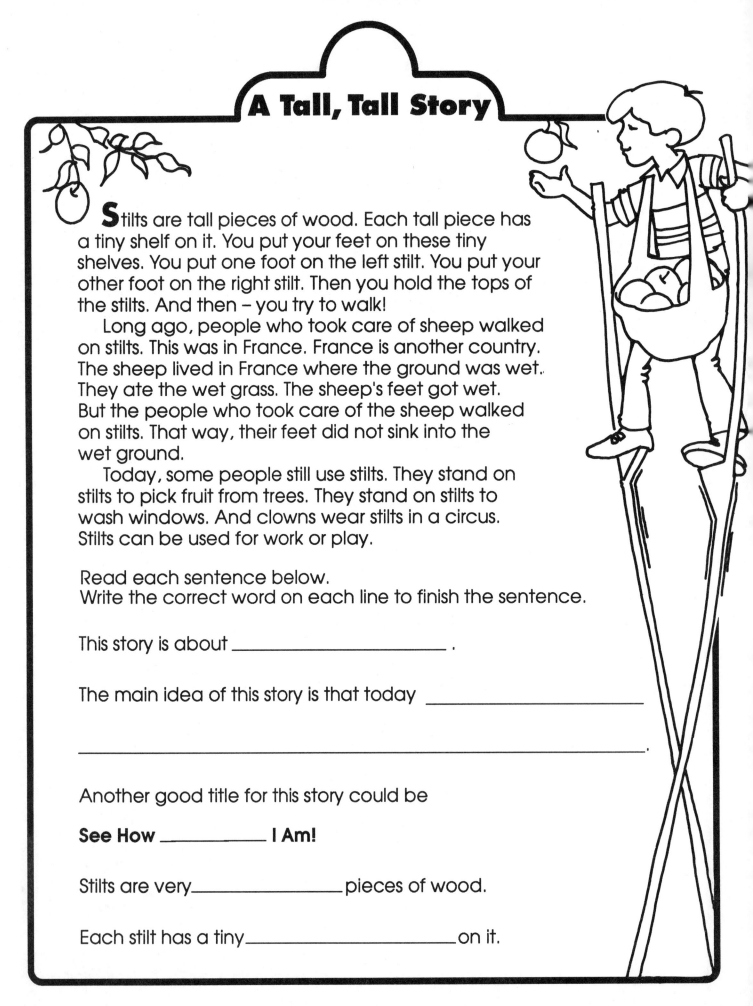

A Tall, Tall Story

Stilts are tall pieces of wood. Each tall piece has a tiny shelf on it. You put your feet on these tiny shelves. You put one foot on the left stilt. You put your other foot on the right stilt. Then you hold the tops of the stilts. And then – you try to walk!

Long ago, people who took care of sheep walked on stilts. This was in France. France is another country. The sheep lived in France where the ground was wet. They ate the wet grass. The sheep's feet got wet. But the people who took care of the sheep walked on stilts. That way, their feet did not sink into the wet ground.

Today, some people still use stilts. They stand on stilts to pick fruit from trees. They stand on stilts to wash windows. And clowns wear stilts in a circus. Stilts can be used for work or play.

Read each sentence below.
Write the correct word on each line to finish the sentence.

This story is about _____ .

The main idea of this story is that today _____

_____ .

Another good title for this story could be

See How _____ I Am!

Stilts are very_____ pieces of wood.

Each stilt has a tiny_____on it.

The Fox and the Ox

Words that rhyme have the same last sound.
Do, **shoe**, and **blue** all rhyme.

Write in the missing words to finish the story.
Write in the word that rhymes with the **bold** word.

you　　　　**box**　　　　**blocks**　　　　**door**　　　　**better**

"I spell my name **f o x**," said **Fox**.

"I spell my name with just three _____ ."

"I do not need a fourth **letter**.

Having only three is _____ ."

"I am smart. I can spell cat, dog, and **fox**.

They rhyme with bat, log, and _____ ."

The ox said, "If three is better than **four**,

Then I will throw one letter out the _____ ."

"I can spell my name with just **two**,

So that makes me smarter than _____ ."

It's Dark Inside

Turtle opened one eye. Dark. It was very dark. Turtle opened her other eye. It was still dark. Why was it dark? Turtle didn't remember where she was.

Turtle could hardly move. Her head was resting on one of her front feet. She moved the front foot. Her other front foot was all folded up. Her two back feet were folded up.

It was dark and there was hardly any room. Oh, yes! Now Turtle remembered. She was all inside her shell!

Turtle slowly pushed her head out. Wow! It was bright. There was sunshine all over.

She slowly pushed each foot out. One, two, three, four. Now Turtle was ready to go.

Slowly, Turtle walked down to the river. She ate a bug on the way. She ate some grass, too.

Oh, oh! What was that sound? It was a dog or a fox!

Turtle pulled her head back into her shell. She pulled her feet in, too.

Outside, she saw a red fox. It tried to bite her shell. Ha! Her shell was very hard. No fox could bite it.

Turtle stayed inside her shell. The fox went away.

Then Turtle put her head and feet out. She went down to the river.

42

Circle **True** if a sentence is true.
Circle **False** if it is not true.

True	**False**	A dog tries to bite Turtle.
True	**False**	Turtle is going to the river.
True	**False**	Turtle eats a bug.
True	**False**	This story is about a fox and a dog.
True	**False**	Another good title for this story is **Safe Inside a Shell**.
True	**False**	**Folded** means **wet**.
True	**False**	When you **bite** something, you put your teeth into it.
True	**False**	First Turtle sees the fox, then she hears it.
True	**False**	Turtles can move very fast.
True	**False**	A turtle's shell keeps it safe from other animals.

The Octopus

The octopus lives in the sea. Octopuses live in seas all over the world. Some octopuses are very small. Some are large. They can be three feet long.

An octopus has a very large head. It has two eyes. Inside the head is a large brain. This means that an octopus can learn. The head is the center of the octopus's body. Around the head are eight arms.

An octopus lives alone, in the crack of a rock. It can squeeze itself into a very small space. This helps it hide from larger animals. Another thing that helps it hide is ink. If something is chasing an octopus, the octopus squirts black ink. The animal chasing it can't see anything but ink.

An octopus hunts for food in the ocean. It eats shellfish. The octopus is a fast hunter. It is a strong hunter, too. When an octopus sees a shellfish, it jumps on top of the shell! Then it pulls open the shell with its strong arms.

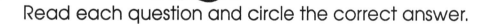

Read each question and circle the correct answer.

Where do octopuses live?

      sand   sea   ink

What is at the center of an octopus's body?

      eyes   arms   head

What do octopuses eat?

      ink   arms   shellfish

How do they get away from other animals?

      They squirt ink.   They jump.   They hunt.

How can an octopus hide?

      It can jump.   It can squeeze into cracks.   It can eat.

Seven Sheep

One day seven sheep wanted to play.

"Let's play a game," said the first sheep. "Let's play follow the leader. I will be the leader first. I will skip across this bridge." The first sheep skipped and the other six sheep followed.

Then it was the second sheep's turn. It ran up a hill and the other six sheep followed. Then the third sheep rolled down the hill and the other sheep followed.

When it was the fourth sheep's turn, it jumped into a large pile of hay. The other six sheep followed.

The fifth sheep was covered with hay. So it ran through a waterfall to get clean. The other sheep followed.

"I will leap over the fence," said the sixth sheep. And so it did. It leaped over the fence and the other sheep followed.

Finally it was the seventh sheep's turn. The seventh sheep found a soft spot in the grass. It lay down on the soft spot. It went to sleep. So did the other sheep.

What does each word mean?
Write the letter of the correct answer next to the word.

_____ **leader**	**a.** water that falls from a high place
_____ **waterfall**	**b.** someone who goes first
_____ **leap**	**c.** to come after or go after
_____ **skip**	**d.** jump
_____ **follow**	**e.** to step and hop

Row, Row, Row Your Boat

Rabbit went down to the river. There were two blue boats in the water. They looked the same. Rabbit got into one of the boats. He began to row down the river. What fun!

Rabbit sang as he rowed. "Row, row, row your boat," he sang. Those were the only words Rabbit knew. That is why he sang them over and over.

Rabbit looked up the river. He saw Brave Bear. Brave Bear was rowing down the river. Brave Bear was rowing the other blue boat very fast.

"Row, row, row your boat," sang Rabbit. He watched Brave Bear row. Soon Brave Bear was even with Rabbit.

"Stop!" shouted Brave Bear.

"Row, row, row your boat," sang Rabbit.

Brave Bear put a paw on Rabbit's boat. "Yes," said Brave Bear. "You can row, row, row *your* boat. But that is *my* boat you are rowing."

Rabbit looked at his boat. It looked like his own blue boat. But then, Brave Bear's boat looked the same. "How can you tell?" asked Rabbit.

"What is in the front of the boat?" asked Brave Bear.

Rabbit looked at the front of the boat. Honey. There were many jars of honey in the boat.

"See," said Brave Bear. "Now, what is in the front of this blue boat?"

Rabbit looked. There were carrots in the front of Brave Bear's blue boat. So Rabbit gave Brave Bear back his boat.

"Row, row, row *my* boat," sang Rabbit as he rowed down the river.

Write an **X** by the answer that tells why something happened.

Why does Brave Bear shout, "Stop?"

_____ Brave Bear does not like blue boats.

_____ Rabbit has taken Brave Bear's blue boat.

_____ Brave Bear rows very fast.

How can Brave Bear tell which boat is his?

_____ The boats are different colors.

_____ His boat is red.

_____ His boat has honey in the front.

Why did Rabbit take the wrong boat?

_____ The boats looked alike.

_____ Rabbit likes the color blue.

_____ Rabbit did not like Brave Bear.

Why does Rabbit sing only "Row, row, row your boat?"

_____ He does not know the rest of the words.

_____ He does not like the rest of the words.

_____ Singing makes him row faster.

At the end, why does Rabbit row the boat that has carrots in it?

_____ Rabbit does not like honey.

_____ The boat with carrots is his boat.

_____ The boat with carrots is orange.

At the end, why does Rabbit sing, "Row, row, row my boat?"

_____ He knows all the words.

_____ Brave Bear likes those words the best.

_____ Rabbit is in his own boat.

Otter's mother taught him many things. She taught him all about the water. She taught him how to swim. His mother taught him how to dive for fish. Otter really liked diving for fish. He liked eating them even more.

That's not all. Otter's mother taught him all about the land, too. He learned how to catch snakes and frogs. Otters are very long animals. They have short legs and are close to the ground. So it was easy for Otter to move along the ground quickly. It was easy for him to catch snakes and frogs.

Now his mother wanted to teach him something new. Otter wasn't sure he would like it. Something strange had happened to the land. It was covered with white powder. The powder was cold. Otter's mother went to the top of a hill. Zoom! She slid down the hill on her belly! Now she waited at the bottom of the hill. Otter knew it was his turn to do the same thing. Would he like it?

Read each question.
Answer each question with a sentence.

Where do otters live? _____

What is the white powder? _____

Who teaches young animals what to do? _____

_____

What does Otter's mother do that shows she likes to play?

_____

Why would it be hard for a tall animal like a giraffe to catch snakes

and frogs? _____

Do You Have Change for a Cow?

Long ago, people did not use money. They did not have pennies or nickels. They did not have dimes or quarters.

There was no money anywhere. So people did not pay for what they wanted. Suppose that Jane wanted shoes. There was no money, so how could Jane get the shoes? Here is how. Jane would trade for the shoes. To trade is to give somebody one thing if that person gives you another thing.

People traded things. Jane traded what she had for what she wanted. Suppose Jane had honey. But she wanted shoes. The person who had shoes wanted honey. So Jane and the other person would trade honey for shoes.

After a long time, animals were used like money. A cow was worth just so much. After animals came corn. It was used like money. Then came sea shells. At long last, somebody made money out of metal. They made coins like we have today. It's a lot easier to carry coins than to carry a cow.

Read each sentence below.
Write the correct word on each line to finish the sentence.

This story is about _____.

The main idea of this story is that long ago people did not

_____.

Another good title for this story could be

Different Kinds of _____.

Before people had coins, they would _____

for what they wanted.

Why do people use money today? _____

_____

Shooting Stars

Have you ever heard of shooting stars? Sometimes you can see them at night. They move across the sky very fast. A trail of light glows behind them. Shooting stars are beautiful to see. But they are not really stars.

A shooting star is a piece of rock from outer space. For many years, the rock spins around in space. When it is out there, in space, it doesn't glow. It has no trail of light.

But as the rock spins, it comes closer and closer to Earth. One day, it comes so close that it falls through our air.

The rock falls very, very fast. As it falls, it makes heat. This heat makes the rock burn. The trail of light is really fire. If the rock falls at night, you can see it burning in the sky. It looks like a bright star that is falling. That is why it is called a shooting star.

Some shooting stars burn themselves up. There is nothing left. But some hit the ground before they burn up. Then the rock makes a hole in the ground.

Read each question.
Write an **X** next to the sentence that answers it.

What happens before the rock falls through our air?

_____ It spins around in space.

_____ It makes a hole in the ground.

What happens before the rock burns away?

_____ It makes a hole in the ground.

_____ It comes very close to Earth and begins to fall.

What happens after the rock comes very close to Earth?

_____ It falls through the air.

_____ It spins around in space.

What happens as the rock falls?

_____ It comes very close to Earth.

_____ It burns.

Do You Believe It?

"**L**ook at that corn!" said Richard. "It's really growing fast."

"It sure is," said his cousin Tanya. Tanya lived on a farm. Richard was from the city. "Corn grows fast in hot weather," she said.

"It sure has been hot," Richard said. He added more ice to his lemonade. "Is it always this hot in the country?"

"Oh, this is nothing," said Tanya. "Last summer it was much hotter. Last summer, it was so hot that the corn in the fields started to pop. It popped right in the field! Big white puffy pieces of corn fell everywhere."

"Really?" asked Richard.

"Sure," answered Tanya. "The pigs and cows saw the big puffy pieces of corn. They thought it was snow. They thought they were in a blizzard! They got so cold that they froze to death."

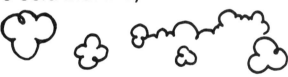

Circle **True** if a sentence is most likely true.
Circle **False** if it is most likely false.
Write a sentence to answer the last question.

True **False** Tanya is telling Richard a true story.

True **False** When it gets cold, it snows popcorn.

True **False** Tanya is having fun with Richard.

True **False** This story is mainly about cows and pigs.

Why could the title of this story be "Tanya's Joke"?_____

_____

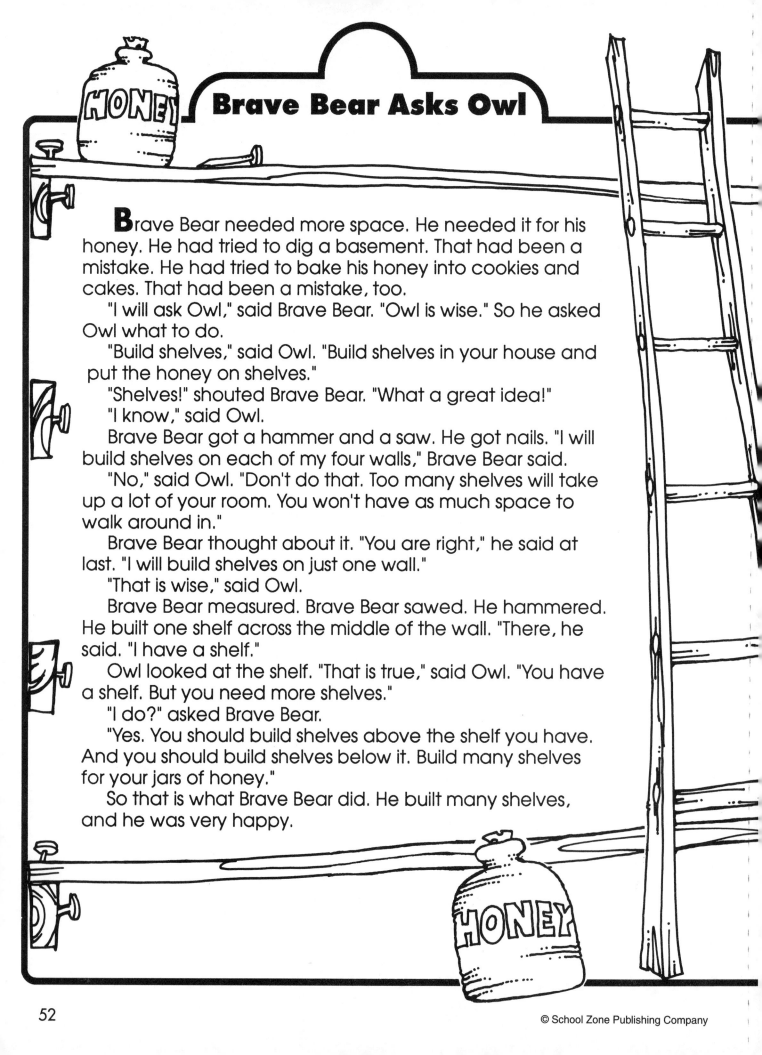

Brave Bear Asks Owl

Brave Bear needed more space. He needed it for his honey. He had tried to dig a basement. That had been a mistake. He had tried to bake his honey into cookies and cakes. That had been a mistake, too.

"I will ask Owl," said Brave Bear. "Owl is wise." So he asked Owl what to do.

"Build shelves," said Owl. "Build shelves in your house and put the honey on shelves."

"Shelves!" shouted Brave Bear. "What a great idea!"

"I know," said Owl.

Brave Bear got a hammer and a saw. He got nails. "I will build shelves on each of my four walls," Brave Bear said.

"No," said Owl. "Don't do that. Too many shelves will take up a lot of your room. You won't have as much space to walk around in."

Brave Bear thought about it. "You are right," he said at last. "I will build shelves on just one wall."

"That is wise," said Owl.

Brave Bear measured. Brave Bear sawed. He hammered. He built one shelf across the middle of the wall. "There, he said. "I have a shelf."

Owl looked at the shelf. "That is true," said Owl. "You have a shelf. But you need more shelves."

"I do?" asked Brave Bear.

"Yes. You should build shelves above the shelf you have. And you should build shelves below it. Build many shelves for your jars of honey."

So that is what Brave Bear did. He built many shelves, and he was very happy.

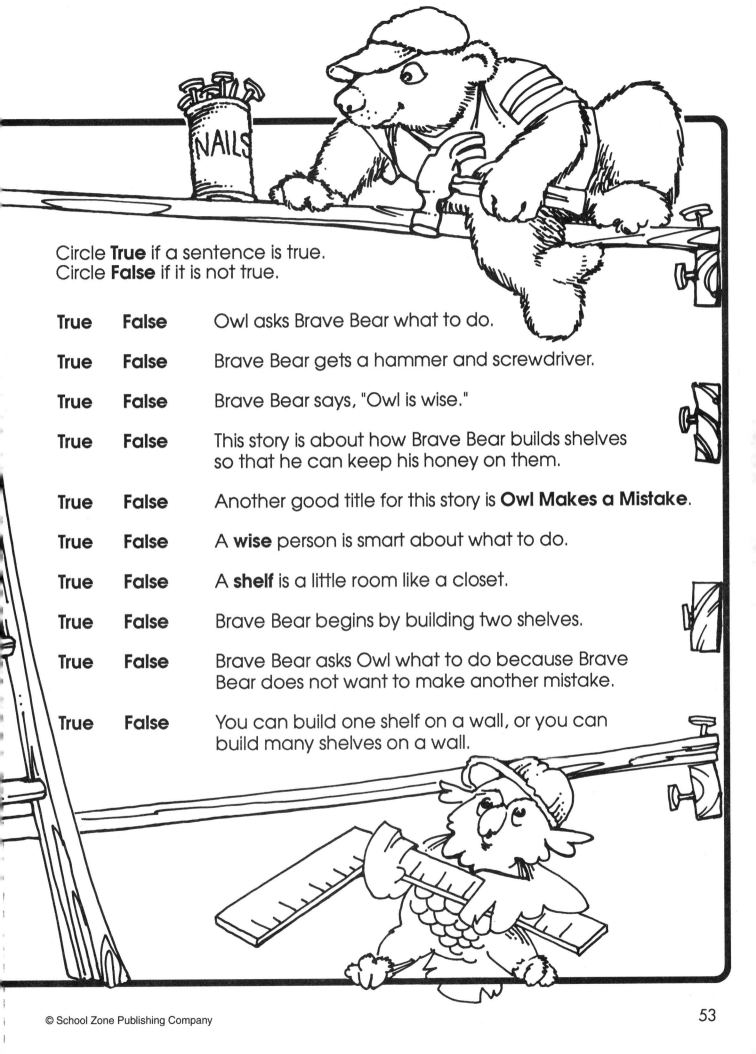

Circle **True** if a sentence is true.
Circle **False** if it is not true.

True   **False**   Owl asks Brave Bear what to do.

True   **False**   Brave Bear gets a hammer and screwdriver.

True   **False**   Brave Bear says, "Owl is wise."

True   **False**   This story is about how Brave Bear builds shelves so that he can keep his honey on them.

True   **False**   Another good title for this story is **Owl Makes a Mistake**.

True   **False**   A **wise** person is smart about what to do.

True   **False**   A **shelf** is a little room like a closet.

True   **False**   Brave Bear begins by building two shelves.

True   **False**   Brave Bear asks Owl what to do because Brave Bear does not want to make another mistake.

True   **False**   You can build one shelf on a wall, or you can build many shelves on a wall.

Name That Finger

Each finger of your hand has a name. It's not a name like Suzie or Chad or Larry. It's a name like *thumb*.

Yes, thumb is the name of one of the five fingers. The thumb is the finger that sticks out to the side. You can touch each of your other four fingers with your thumb. That's because the thumb moves in a different direction.

The finger next to the thumb is called the index finger. You use this finger to flip through a pile of papers one at a time.

After that comes the middle finger. There are two fingers before it and two after it. This is why it's called the middle finger.

Next to the middle finger is the ring finger. It is called the ring finger because people often wear a ring on this finger.

The last finger has two names. Some people call it the little finger. Other people call it the pinkie.

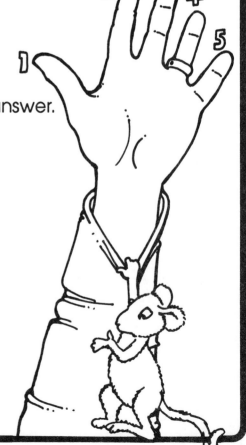

Look at the numbers on the drawing.
Read each question and circle the correct answer.

What is the name of finger number 3?

ring   **middle**   **index**

What is the name of finger number 5?

tiny   **thumb**   **pinkie**

What is the name of finger number 2?

middle   **index**   **little**

What is the name of finger number 4?

ring   **index**   **pinkie**

Which animal has hands like ours?

frog   **monkey**   **dog**

Brave Bear Sorts Honey

Brave Bear was very happy with his new shelves. "I will put my honey on the shelves," he said.

Brave Bear looked around. He had many, many jars of honey. Some jars were full of dark-colored honey. Sage honey was dark. And buckwheat was dark. "I love dark honey," said Brave Bear, licking his lips. "It tastes so sweet!"

More of the jars were full of light-colored honey. Clover honey was light. Linden honey was also light. So was orange honey. And lavender honey was also light in color. "I love light honey," said Brave Bear, opening a jar. "It tastes so sweet!"

Brave Bear ate some honey and looked at the jars. "I must sort these jars," he said. "I must have a plan."

Brave Bear thought about it. "I know," he said. "I will put all my dark honey on the left-hand shelves. And I will put all my light honey on the right-hand shelves." And so he did.

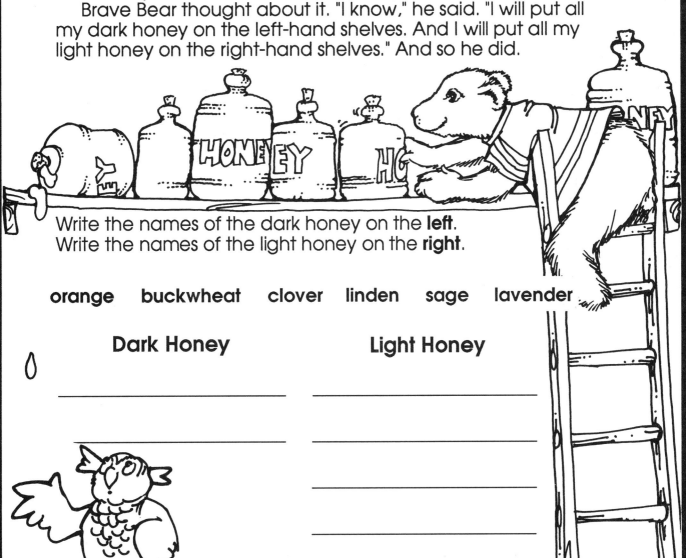

Write the names of the dark honey on the **left**.
Write the names of the light honey on the **right**.

orange   buckwheat   clover   linden   sage   lavender

Dark Honey	Light Honey
_____	_____
_____	_____
	_____
	_____

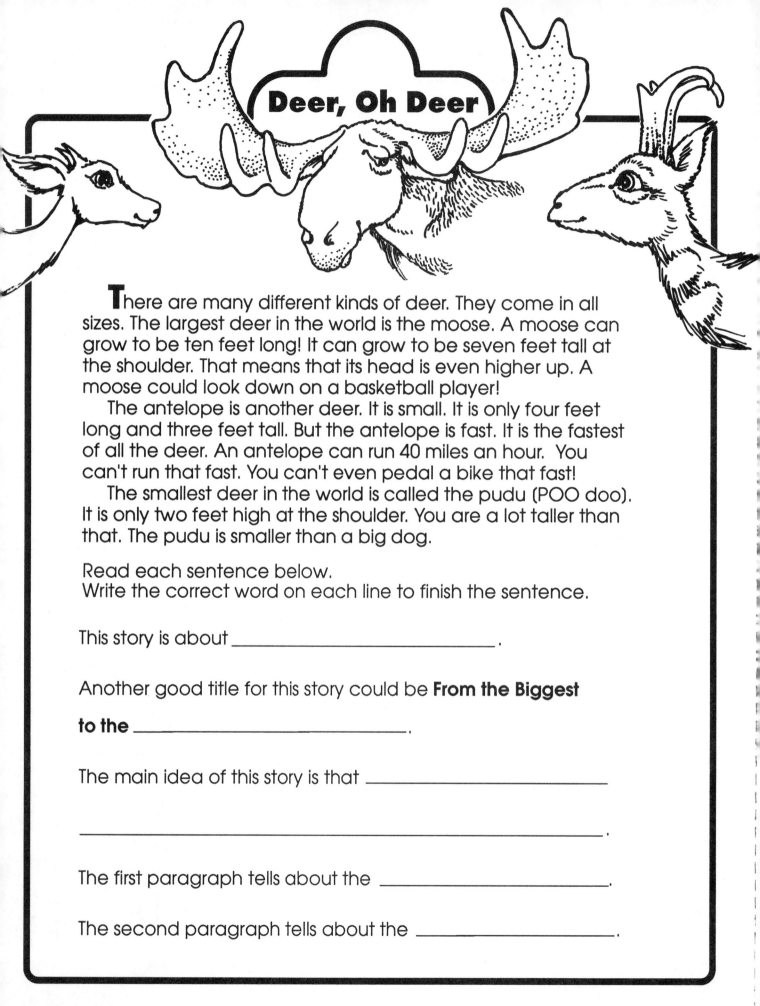

Deer, Oh Deer

There are many different kinds of deer. They come in all sizes. The largest deer in the world is the moose. A moose can grow to be ten feet long! It can grow to be seven feet tall at the shoulder. That means that its head is even higher up. A moose could look down on a basketball player!

The antelope is another deer. It is small. It is only four feet long and three feet tall. But the antelope is fast. It is the fastest of all the deer. An antelope can run 40 miles an hour. You can't run that fast. You can't even pedal a bike that fast!

The smallest deer in the world is called the pudu (POO doo). It is only two feet high at the shoulder. You are a lot taller than that. The pudu is smaller than a big dog.

Read each sentence below.
Write the correct word on each line to finish the sentence.

This story is about _____.

Another good title for this story could be **From the Biggest**

to the _____.

The main idea of this story is that _____

_____.

The first paragraph tells about the _____.

The second paragraph tells about the _____.

56

Greenland Is Not Green

GREENLAND

NORTH AMERICA

SOUTH AMERICA

Greenland is the largest island in the world. It is way north, in the cold ocean. Near Greenland is another island. It is small. Its name is Iceland.

Do you think that Greenland is green and warm? Do you think that Iceland is white and cold? If you do, you are wrong.

Not many people live on the big island of Greenland. There might be more people in your town than in all of Greenland. That is because Greenland is not green. Greenland is white. Most of the island is covered with ice – lots and lots of ice. The ice that covers Greenland is higher than the world's tallest building.

Greenland is also foggy. There is so much fog that boats and planes have trouble finding Greenland.

What about Iceland? Is it colder than Greenland? No, it is not.

Iceland has ice, but not as much ice as Greenland. Iceland has a lot of hot springs. A spring is a hole in the ground that fills with water. The water in Iceland's ground is very hot. The land is not as cold as Greenland. And there are a lot more people who live in Iceland.

Answer each question with a sentence.

What are Greenland and Iceland? _____

Why is Greenland not green? _____
_____

Why do planes and boats have trouble finding Greenland? _____
_____

Which island has more people? _____

Why do more people live on the smaller island? _____
_____

Penguins

Penguins are black and white birds. Penguins do not stand like other birds. They stand up straight, like a person does. When they walk, they walk very, very slowly.

They have wings, but penguins do not use their wings to fly. Penguins cannot fly. Instead, they swim. They use their wings like flippers. They use them to move in the water. When penguins swim, they swim very fast. Of all the birds that swim underwater, penguins swim the fastest.

Penguins can walk, and penguins can swim. There is one other way that penguins can move. If it wants to go down a hill, a penguin gets on its belly. Then it slides down the hill. That is much faster than walking.

Read each sentence below.
Write the correct word on each line to finish the sentence.

This story is about _____.

Another good title for this story could be

How_____**Move**.

The main idea of this story is that   _____

_____.

The second paragraph tells how penguins _____.

The third paragraph tells how penguins _____.

The Olympics

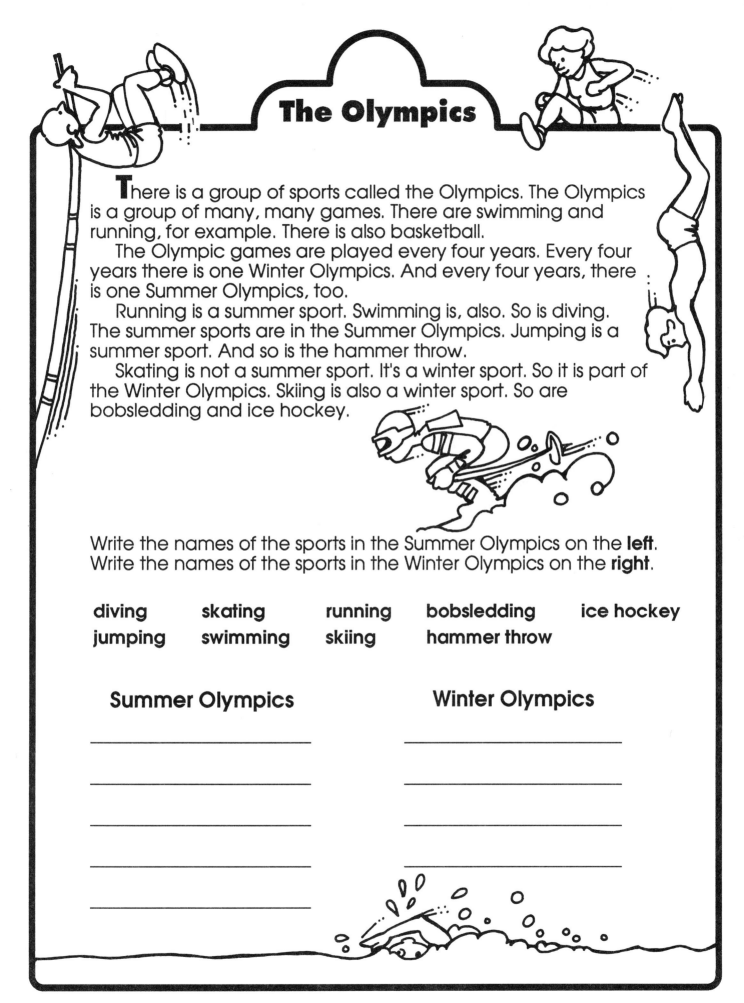

There is a group of sports called the Olympics. The Olympics is a group of many, many games. There are swimming and running, for example. There is also basketball.

The Olympic games are played every four years. Every four years there is one Winter Olympics. And every four years, there is one Summer Olympics, too.

Running is a summer sport. Swimming is, also. So is diving. The summer sports are in the Summer Olympics. Jumping is a summer sport. And so is the hammer throw.

Skating is not a summer sport. It's a winter sport. So it is part of the Winter Olympics. Skiing is also a winter sport. So are bobsledding and ice hockey.

Write the names of the sports in the Summer Olympics on the **left**.
Write the names of the sports in the Winter Olympics on the **right**.

diving   skating   running   bobsledding   ice hockey
jumping   swimming   skiing   hammer throw

Summer Olympics

_____

_____

_____

_____

_____

Winter Olympics

_____

_____

_____

_____

Brave Bear Naps

Brave Bear walked through the woods. Way up in the sky, he could see the sun. It was way above the tree tops. But down here in the forest, it was dark and cool.

Up ahead was a berry bush. Brave Bear smelled the bush. Yum. He sat down in front of the bush. He ate the berries, every last one of them. "Those were good berries," said Brave Bear.

Brave Bear came to the river. He drank some water. The cold water tasted good. Then Brave Bear jumped into the river. The cold water felt good. He swam and swam. He even ate a few fish.

After he got out of the river, Brave Bear walked up a hill. He saw a bee. "If I follow the bee," said Brave Bear, "I will find honey." So he followed the bee and found the beehive. Of course Brave Bear ate the honey.

"I am tired," said Brave Bear. "I will take a nap." So he found a soft spot beside a log. He curled up. And he took a long nap.

Write a sentence to answer each question.

Why is it dark and cool in the forest? _____

_____

Why did Brave Bear follow the bee? _____

_____

Why was it a good idea for Brave Bear to follow the bee?

_____

What would it be like to be a bear for one day?

_____

_____

They Go Together

A pair is two things that go together. A salt shaker and pepper shaker are a pair. A left shoe and a right shoe are also a pair.

People can also be a pair. A mother and father are a pair. Two brothers are a pair. Two sisters are a pair. A brother and a sister are also a pair. Batman and Robin are a pair.

Can you think of some famous pairs in stories? These are people or animals who go together. Think of a brother and sister in a forest. That pair is Hansel and Gretel. Think of two children who go up a hill. Who is the pair? It's Jack and Jill, of course.

Now think about cartoons. Who are the squirrel and the moose that make a pair? It's Rocky and Bullwinkle. A little bear and a big bear live in Jellystone Park. Who is this famous pair? It's Boo Boo and Yogi Bear.

There are many famous pairs. How many can you think of?

Circle **True** if a sentence is most likely true.
Circle **False** if it is most likely false.
Write sentences to answer the last two questions.

True   **False**   Only real live people can be pairs.

True   **False**   Superman and Lois Lane are a pair.

True   **False**   A man and a salt shaker are a pair.

Name two things that are **not** a pair. _____

Name some pairs that aren't in the story. _____

_____

Brave Bear Teaches

Owl was teaching the animals about other animals. "I will teach you about the dog family," said Owl.

"There are many animals in the dog family. First, there is the wolf. It belongs to the dog family. Then there is the coyote. It also belongs. And so does the fox."

"That is nice," said Brave Bear.

Owl said, "There is the jackal. The jackal belongs to the dog family. And of course, there is the dog. It belongs to the dog family."

Owl looked at Brave Bear. "I wonder," said Owl, "if the bear belongs to the dog family. Is the bear just a large dog without a tail?"

Brave Bear stood up. "No!" he shouted. "The bear is not a dog! Bears belong to the bear family!"

"The brown bear belongs to this family. So does the black bear. And so does the polar bear." Brave Bear was not done. "The sun bear belongs to the bear family. So does the sloth bear. Bears are bears," said Brave Bear. "We are not dogs."

Write the names of the animals in the **Dog Family** on the **left**.
Write the names of the animals in the **Bear Family** on the **right**.

sun	wolf	jackal	sloth	brown
fox	black	coyote	polar	dog

Dog Family

_____

_____

_____

_____

Bear Family

_____

_____

_____

_____

62

Page 33
house
door
bed
pet
honey

Page 34
Rabbit
sound
ears
Mother

Page 35
trees
there are many different
kinds of trees.
Trees
leaves
biggest

Page 36
bedroom
yes
Owl
space
honey

Page 37
log
bone
luck
jog
truck

Page 38
plant
cornmeal
yellow
cob
pop

Page 39
e
d
a
c
b

Page 40
stilts
people use stilts
for work or play.
Tall
tall – long – high
shelf

Page 41
blocks
better
box
door
you

Pages 42 & 43
False
True
True
False
True
False
True
False
False
True

Page 44
sea
head
shellfish
They squirt ink.
It can squeeze into cracks.

Page 45
b
a
d
e
c

Pages 46 & 47
Rabbit has taken Brave Bear's blue boat.
His boat has honey in the front.
The boats looked alike.
He does not know the rest of the words.
The boat with carrots is his boat.
Rabbit is in his own boat.

Page 48
Otters live on land and water.
It is snow.
Their mothers teach young animals what to do.
She slides down a hill in the snow.
Tall animals would have a hard time bending close to the ground.

Page 49
money – trade
Use money to buy things.
Money – Trading
trade
Money is easy to carry and use.

Page 50
It spins around in space.
It comes very close to Earth and begins to fall.
It falls through the air.
It burns.

Page 51
False
False
True
False
Tanya is pulling a joke on Richard.

Pages 52 & 53
False
False
True
True
False
True
False
False
True
True

Page 54
middle
pinkie
index
ring
monkey

Page 55
Dark Honey
sage
buckwheat
Light Honey
orange
clover
linden
lavender

Page 56
deer
Smallest or Littlest
There are many different kinds of deer.
moose
antelope

Page 57
They are islands.
It is covered with ice.
There is fog all around it.
Iceland has more people.
More people live on Iceland
because it is warmer than Greenland.

Page 58
penguins
Penguins
penguins move in three ways.
swim
slide

Page 59
Summer Olympics
diving
running
jumping
swimming
hammer throw
Winter Olympics
skating
bobsledding
ice hockey
skiing

Page 60
It is dark and cool in the forest because the trees keep out most of the sun.
Brave Bear follows the bee so that the bee will lead him to honey.
It is a good idea for Brave Bear to follow the bee because the bee leads him to honey.
Answers will vary.

Page 61
False
True
False
Answers will vary.
Answers will vary.

Page 62

Dog Family	Bear Family
wolf	sun
jackal	sloth
fox	brown
coyote	black
dog	polar

COUNT DOWN

Write the numbers 1-20

COUNT BY TEN

Fill in the path below by counting by tens to 100.

START

THIS WAY TO THE COUNTING PATH

NUMBERS OF TENS AND ONES

Numbers can be put in sets of tens and ones.

74 = 7 tens + 4 ones
        70 + 4

44 = 4 tens + 4 ones
        40 + 4

Putting numbers in sets of tens and ones is called EXPANDED NOTATION.

Try it.

1. 78 = _____ tens + _____ ones
       _____ + _____

2. 34 = _____ tens + _____ ones
       _____ + _____

3. 67 = _____ tens + _____ ones
       _____ + _____

4. 46 = _____ tens + _____ ones
       _____ + _____

5. 27 = _____ tens + _____ ones
       _____ + _____

WHAT IS AN ABACUS?

This is an abacus. → → These are spindles.

We can show any number 0-9 by putting counters on the (ones) spindle.

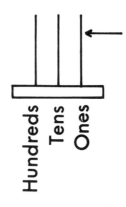

← Spindles

Hundreds Tens Ones

 = **3**

What number is shown on this abacus? _____

The answer is 5.

Write the correct numeral.	Place the correct number of counters on the (ones) spindle.
1.  = _____	5. **8** =
2. = _____	6. **5** =
3. = _____	7. **7** =
4. 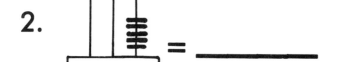 = _____	8. **9** =

TENS ON AN ABACUS

The middle spindle shows the tens place.

We can now show larger numbers using the abacus. **13** =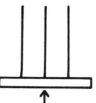

Show 15 on the abacus.

This is 15.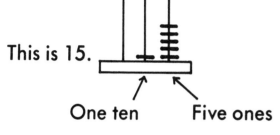

One ten   Five ones

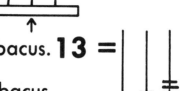

Write the correct numeral.

1. = _____

2. = _____

3. = _____

4. = _____

5. = _____

Place the correct number of counters on the spindles.

6. **17** =

7. **14** =

8. **13** =

9. **19** =

10. **18** =

MORE TENS

Each counter on the tens spindle stands for 10.

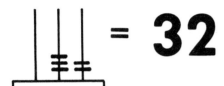 = **32**   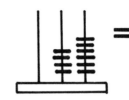 = **46**

| Write the correct numeral. | Place the correct number of counters on the spindles. |

1. 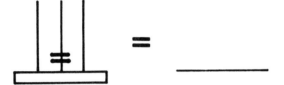 = _____

6. **59** =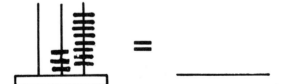

2. 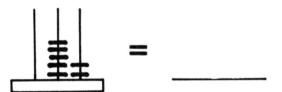 = _____

7. **25** =

3. 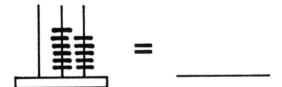 = _____

8. **61** =

4. = _____

9. **40** =

5. 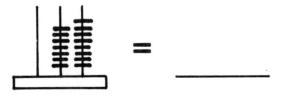 = _____

10. **37** =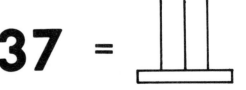

COLUMN ADDITION

Find the sum.

$$\begin{matrix} 2 \\ 3 \\ +6 \end{matrix} \Big\rangle = 5 \quad$$ Add the first two numbers.

$$\begin{matrix} 2 \\ 3 \\ +6 \\ \hline 11 \end{matrix} \quad$$ Add 5 and 6.

REMEMBER: Add the top two numerals first.

1.
$$\begin{matrix} 6 \\ 7 \\ +5 \\ \hline \end{matrix}$$
2.
$$\begin{matrix} 3 \\ 3 \\ +2 \\ \hline \end{matrix}$$
3.
$$\begin{matrix} 7 \\ 4 \\ +6 \\ \hline \end{matrix}$$
4.
$$\begin{matrix} 4 \\ 5 \\ +1 \\ \hline \end{matrix}$$
5.
$$\begin{matrix} 6 \\ 6 \\ +2 \\ \hline \end{matrix}$$

6.
$$\begin{matrix} 3 \\ 4 \\ +5 \\ \hline \end{matrix}$$
7.
$$\begin{matrix} 1 \\ 9 \\ +8 \\ \hline \end{matrix}$$
8.
$$\begin{matrix} 4 \\ 2 \\ +9 \\ \hline \end{matrix}$$
9.
$$\begin{matrix} 5 \\ 5 \\ +4 \\ \hline \end{matrix}$$
10.
$$\begin{matrix} 2 \\ 6 \\ +7 \\ \hline \end{matrix}$$

11.
$$\begin{matrix} 7 \\ 4 \\ +9 \\ \hline \end{matrix}$$
12.
$$\begin{matrix} 8 \\ 8 \\ +2 \\ \hline \end{matrix}$$
13.
$$\begin{matrix} 7 \\ 7 \\ +6 \\ \hline \end{matrix}$$
14.
$$\begin{matrix} 8 \\ 3 \\ +9 \\ \hline \end{matrix}$$
15.
$$\begin{matrix} 7 \\ 3 \\ +9 \\ \hline \end{matrix}$$

MORE SUMS

Find the sums.

$$\begin{array}{r} 2\fbox{1} \\ +\fbox{5} \\ \hline \fbox{6} \end{array}$$

Always add the ones first.

$$\begin{array}{r} \fbox{2}1 \\ +5 \\ \hline \fbox{2}6 \end{array}$$

Then add the tens.

Fill in the blanks.

A. Always add the _____ column first.

B. Add the _____ column next.

---

1. $\begin{array}{r} 22 \\ +5 \\ \hline \end{array}$

2. $\begin{array}{r} 76 \\ +3 \\ \hline \end{array}$

3. $\begin{array}{r} 34 \\ +2 \\ \hline \end{array}$

4. $\begin{array}{r} 81 \\ +7 \\ \hline \end{array}$

5. $\begin{array}{r} 44 \\ +4 \\ \hline \end{array}$

6. $\begin{array}{r} 57 \\ +1 \\ \hline \end{array}$

7. $\begin{array}{r} 13 \\ +6 \\ \hline \end{array}$

8. $\begin{array}{r} 60 \\ +9 \\ \hline \end{array}$

9. $\begin{array}{r} 91 \\ +8 \\ \hline \end{array}$

10. $\begin{array}{r} 55 \\ +4 \\ \hline \end{array}$

TWO DIGIT ADDITION

REMEMBER:

$$\begin{array}{r} 2\boxed{1} \\ + 3\boxed{6} \\ \hline \boxed{7} \end{array}$$ Add the ones first . . . $$\begin{array}{r} \boxed{2}1 \\ + \boxed{3}6 \\ \hline \boxed{5}7 \end{array}$$ then add the tens.

---

1. $$\begin{array}{r} 32 \\ + 12 \\ \hline \end{array}$$

2. $$\begin{array}{r} 62 \\ + 27 \\ \hline \end{array}$$

3. $$\begin{array}{r} 44 \\ + 44 \\ \hline \end{array}$$

4. $$\begin{array}{r} 71 \\ + 28 \\ \hline \end{array}$$

5. $$\begin{array}{r} 26 \\ + 53 \\ \hline \end{array}$$

6. $$\begin{array}{r} 16 \\ + 83 \\ \hline \end{array}$$

7. $$\begin{array}{r} 50 \\ + 29 \\ \hline \end{array}$$

8. $$\begin{array}{r} 81 \\ + 18 \\ \hline \end{array}$$

9. $$\begin{array}{r} 38 \\ + 51 \\ \hline \end{array}$$

10. $$\begin{array}{r} 67 \\ + 30 \\ \hline \end{array}$$

73

ADDITION OF TENS

How many tens?

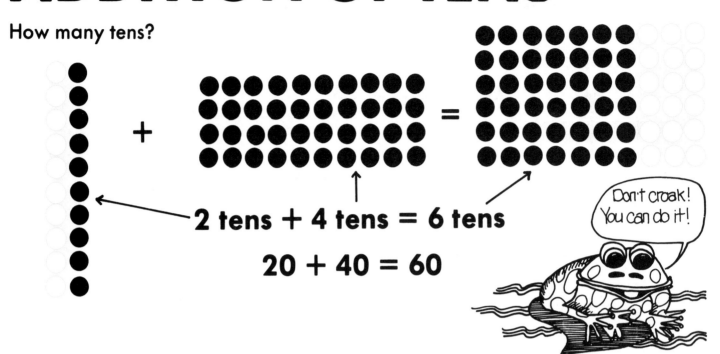

2 tens + 4 tens = 6 tens

20 + 40 = 60

Don't croak! You can do it!

1. 6 tens + 2 tens = _____ tens   60 + 20 = _____

2. 2 tens + 4 tens = _____ tens   20 + 40 = _____

3. 3 tens + 3 tens = _____ tens   30 + 30 = _____

4. 5 tens + 1 ten = _____ tens   50 + 10 = _____

5. 7 tens + 2 tens = _____ tens   70 + 20 = _____

6. 9 tens + 1 ten = _____ tens   90 + 10 = _____

7. 4 tens + 3 tens = _____ tens   40 + 30 = _____

DOES IT EQUAL?

(=) An equal sign means both sides of the equation are the same. They are balanced!

$$6 + 3 = 9$$

Both sides equal 9.

Balance the following equations.

1. $5 + \square = 9$

2. $\square + 2 = 5$

3. $3 + \square = 7$

4. $\square + 4 = 7$

5. $6 + \square = 9$

6. $\square + 2 = 6$

7. $4 + \square = 8$

8. $5 + \square = 7$

PRACTICE TIME

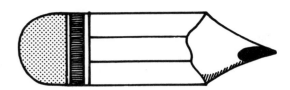

Find the sum.

1.
```
    3
    5
  + 4
  ___
```

2.
```
    6
    7
  + 8
  ___
```

3.
```
    3
    3
  + 4
  ___
```

4.
```
    5
    2
  + 3
  ___
```

5.
```
   13
  + 3
  ___
```

6.
```
   45
  + 2
  ___
```

7.
```
   33
  + 3
  ___
```

8.
```
   60
  + 7
  ___
```

9.
```
   43
  + 56
  ___
```

10.
```
   44
  + 32
  ___
```

11.
```
   56
  + 32
  ___
```

12.
```
   78
  + 21
  ___
```

TAKE AWAY

Find the difference.

12 objects take away 4 = 8 objects left.

1.

_____ - _____ = _____

2.

_____ - _____ = _____

3.

_____ - _____ = _____

4.

_____ - _____ = _____

5.

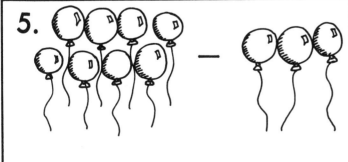

_____ - _____ = _____

6.

_____ - _____ = _____

FIND THE DIFFERENCE

$$\begin{array}{r} 28 \\ -\ 5 \\ \hline 3 \end{array}$$

Always subtract the ones first.

Then subtract the tens.

$$\begin{array}{r} 28 \\ -\ 5 \\ \hline 23 \end{array}$$

Aha!!

The difference is 23.

Do the problems below.

1. $\begin{array}{r} 37 \\ -\ 5 \\ \hline \end{array}$

2. $\begin{array}{r} 54 \\ -\ 3 \\ \hline \end{array}$

3. $\begin{array}{r} 62 \\ -\ 1 \\ \hline \end{array}$

4. $\begin{array}{r} 55 \\ -\ 5 \\ \hline \end{array}$

5. $\begin{array}{r} 44 \\ -\ 2 \\ \hline \end{array}$

6. $\begin{array}{r} 28 \\ -\ 2 \\ \hline \end{array}$

7. $\begin{array}{r} 12 \\ -\ 1 \\ \hline \end{array}$

8. $\begin{array}{r} 79 \\ -\ 6 \\ \hline \end{array}$

9. $\begin{array}{r} 88 \\ -\ 4 \\ \hline \end{array}$

10. $\begin{array}{r} 29 \\ -\ 7 \\ \hline \end{array}$

I knew you could do it!

TWO DIGIT DIFFERENCE

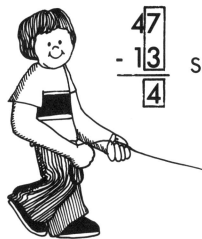

47
- 13
4

Subtract the ones.

- 47
13
34

Subtract the tens.

The difference is 34.

Do the problems below.

1.   48
  - 31

2.   62
  - 11

3.   13
  - 10

4.   37
  - 24

5.   76
  - 52

6.   25
  - 13

7.   81
  - 61

8.   98
  - 75

9.   19
  - 12

10.   46
  - 23

11.   57
  - 36

12.   73
  - 62

13.   38
  - 22

14.   65
  - 43

15.   54
  - 42

Arf arf! (Good work!)

PRACTICE TIME

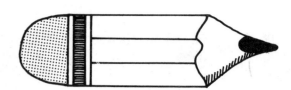

Find the difference.

1. 18
   - 3

2. 14
   - 4

3. 5
   - 3

4. 2
   - 1

5. 9
   - 3

6. 33
   - 21

7. 56
   - 43

8. 62
   - 31

9. 17
   - 6

10. 15
    - 3

11. 4
    - 3

12. 8
    - 5

13. 6
    - 1

14. 43
    - 32

15. 25
    - 14

16. 18
    - 8

17. 34
    - 2

18. 73
    - 41

19. 5
    - 2

20. 9
    - 2

80

Take a break!

SAME SIZE - SAME SHAPE

Look at the shapes below. Each shape has two parts.
Each part is the same size and same shape.

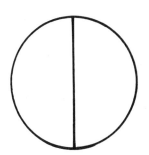 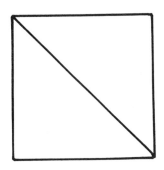

They're both the same!

Put an "X" on the shapes below that have the same size and same shape.

1.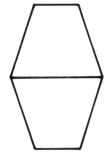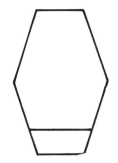

4.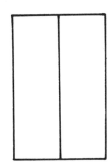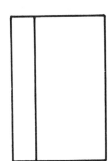

2.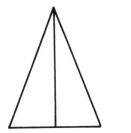

5.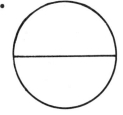

3.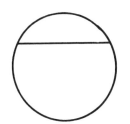

6.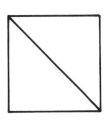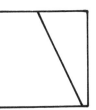

Parts of an object that are the same size and same shape are

CONGRUENT
PARTS.

CONGRUENT SHAPES

Look at the shapes below. Each shape has 2 congruent parts. Each part is ½ or one half.

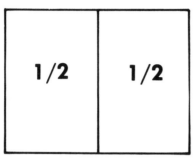

1/2 1/2

1/2 1/2

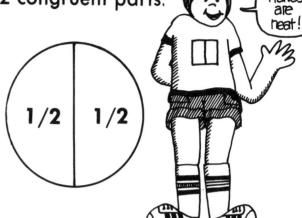

Halves are neat!

Write the fraction ½ in each part.

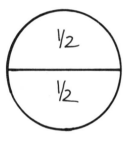

½

½

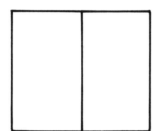

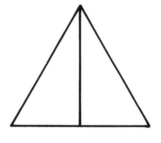

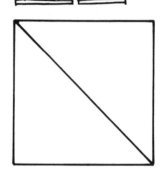

Color ½ of each shape. The first one is done for you.

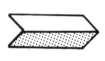

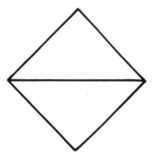

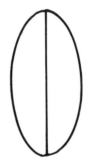

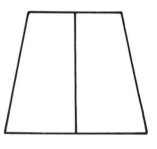

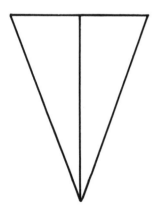

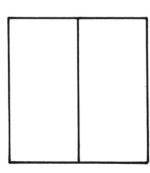

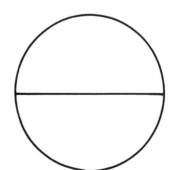

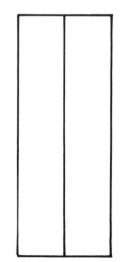

82

SAME SIZE- SAME SHAPE

Look at the shapes below. Each shape has 4 congruent parts.
Each part is the same size and shape.

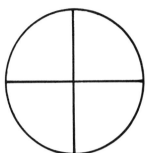  

Draw an "X" on the shapes below that have the same size and same shape.

1.

4.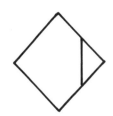

2.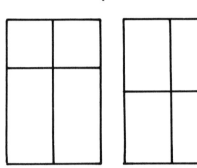

5.

3.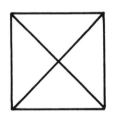

6.

¼ - CONGRUENT

Look at the shapes below. Each object has 4 congruent parts.
Each part is ¼ or one quarter.

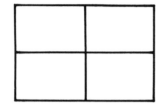

One quarter, two quarters, three quarters, four quarters! Easy!

Write the fraction ¼ in each part of the shape. The first one is done for you.

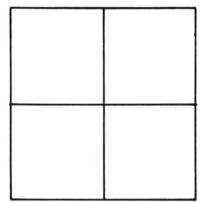

Color ¼ of each shape. The first one is done for you.

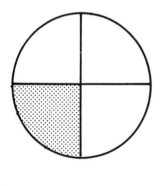

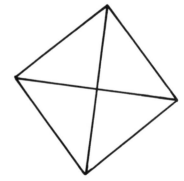

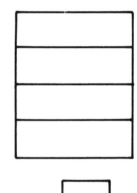

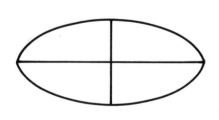

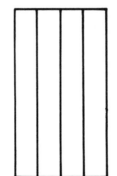

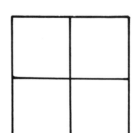

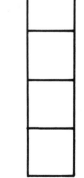

84

WHAT IS A FRACTION?

A fraction tells how many parts are in the whole object.

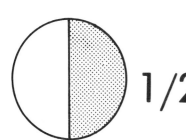 1/2   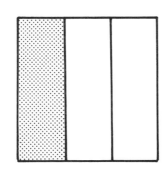 1/3   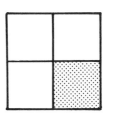 1/4

The bottom number of a fraction tells how many parts in all.

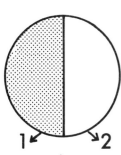

1/2 ← parts in all

Count the parts. Write the number in the box.

1. 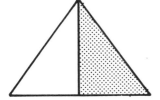 1/☐

2. 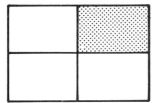 1/☐

3. 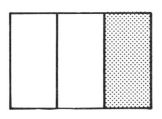 1/☐

4. 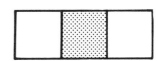 1/☐

5. 1/☐

6. 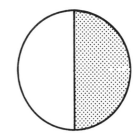 1/☐

MORE FRACTIONS!

A fraction tells how many parts of the whole are being used.
These fractions tell about the shaded part of each shape.

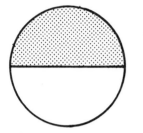 1/2

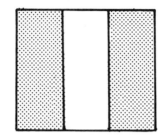 2/3

 3/4

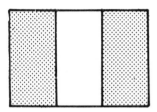 

2/3 → parts are shaded

→ parts in all

Write the correct fraction for each shaded object.

1. 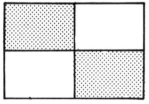 □/4	**4.** 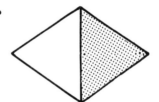 □/2
2. 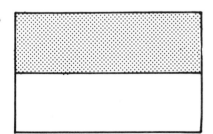 □/2	**5.** 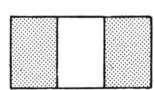 □/3
3. 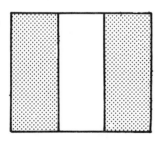 □/3	**6.** 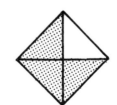 □/4

PICK THE FRACTION

Circle the correct fraction.

1.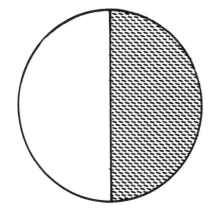

1/2   1/3   1/4

2.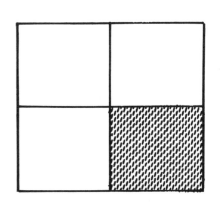

1/2   1/3   1/4

3.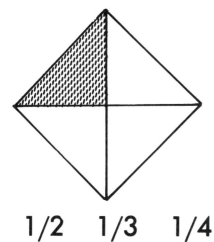

1/2   1/3   1/4

4.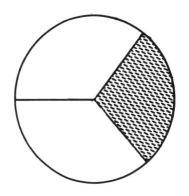

1/2   1/3   1/4

5.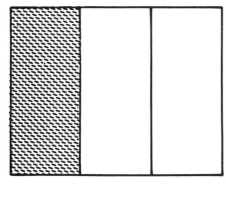

1/2   1/3   1/4

6.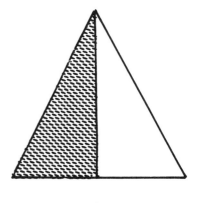

1/2   1/3   1/4

WHAT MONTH IS IT?

A year has 12 months in it. The months are:

1. January
2. February
3. March
4. April
5. May
6. June

7. July
8. August
9. September
10. October
11. November
12. December

On the lines below, write the months of the year in order.

1. _____

2. _____

3. _____

4. _____

5. _____

6. _____

7. _____

8. _____

9. _____

10. _____

11. _____

12. _____

WHAT'S IN A WEEK?

There are seven days in a week. They are:

1. Sunday
2. Monday
3. Tuesday
4. Wednesday

5. Thursday
6. Friday
7. Saturday

On the lines below, write the days of the week.

1. _____   5. _____

2. _____   6. _____

3. _____   7. _____

4. _____

In one day there are 24 hours. The hour hand goes around the clock 2 times to make one day.

How many hours equal one day? _____

WHAT IS THE DAY-DATE?

MAY						
SUN.	**MON.**	**TUE.**	**WED.**	**THU.**	**FRI.**	**SAT.**
		1	2	3	4	5
6	7	8	9	10	11	12
13	14	15	16	17	18	19
20	21	22	23	24	25	26
27	28	29	30	31		

Using the calendar above, answer the following questions.

1. What day of the week does May 15 come on? _____
2. What day of the week does May 5 come on? _____
3. What day of the week does May 23 come on? _____
4. What day of the week does May 20 come on? _____

Unscramble the months of the year.

March, January, June, February, April, October, July, September, May, November, August, December.

1. _____   5. _____   9. _____

2. _____   6. _____   10. _____

3. _____   7. _____   11. _____

4. _____   8. _____   12. _____

THERMOMETER, PLEASE!

When we measure temperature, we use a thermometer.
A thermometer measures how hot or cold it is.
Look at the thermometer.
The temperature on the thermometer is 40 degrees.
This sign ° means degree.
Write the temperature using the ° sign.

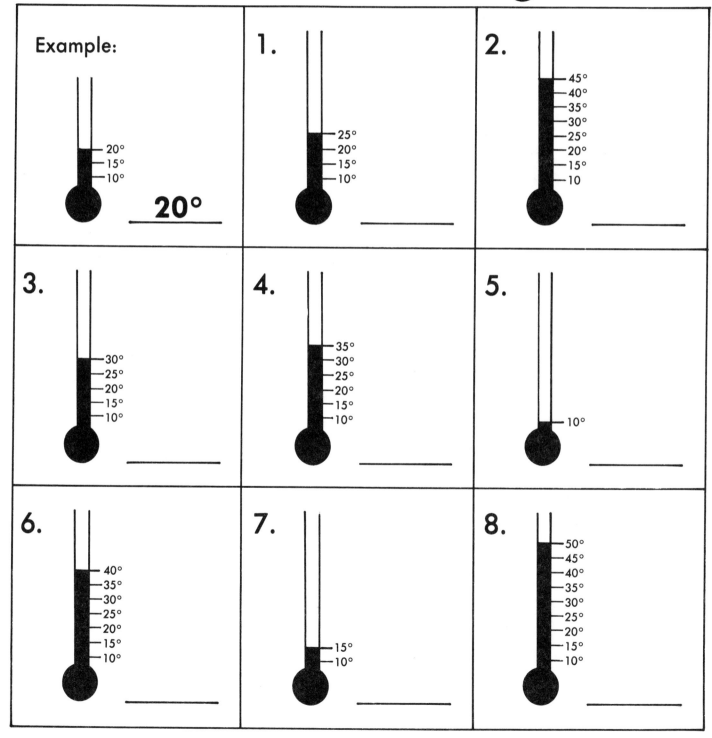

Example: **20°**

1.

2.

3.

4.

5.

6.

7.

8.

MONEY

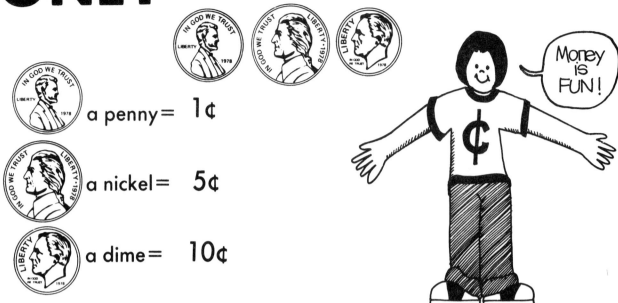

a penny = 1¢

a nickel = 5¢

a dime = 10¢

Money is FUN!

In the problems below, place an "X" on the correct number of coins to equal the amount given.

1. 22¢	
2. 35¢	
3. 17¢	
4. 41¢	

MORE MONEY

 a penny = 1¢   a dime = 10¢

 a nickel = 5¢    a quarter = 25¢

Place an "X" on all the quarters.

1.

Circle the value of the coin in the picture.

2.

    1¢   5¢   10¢   25¢

3.

    1¢   5¢   10¢   25¢

4.

    1¢   5¢   10¢   25¢

5.

    1¢   5¢   10¢   25¢

Write the amount of money shown, using the ¢ sign.

6.

_____

7.

_____

SHAPES

Match the picture to its name.

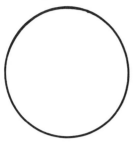

1.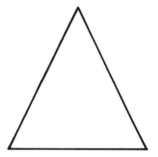

2.

3.

rectangle

triangle

circle

Draw the picture for the shape.

circle	rectangle
triangle	Make a picture using all 3 shapes.

94

Page 65
1, 2, 3, 4,
5, 6, 7, 8,
9, 10, 11, 12,
13, 14, 15, 16,
17, 18, 19, 20

Page 66
10, 20, 30, 40
50, 60, 70, 80
90, 100

Page 67
1. 7 tens + 8 ones – 70 + 8
2. 3 tens + 4 ones – 30 + 4
3. 6 tens + 7 ones – 60 + 7
4. 4 tens + 6 ones – 40 + 6
5. 2 tens + 7 ones – 20 + 7

Page 68
1. 4
2. 5
3. 6
4. 2
5. 8 ones
6. 5 ones
7. 7 ones
8. 9 ones

Page 69
1. 12
2. 15
3. 17
4. 18
5. 11
6. 1 ten 7 ones
7. 1 ten 4 ones
8. 1 ten 3 ones
9. 1 ten 9 ones
10. 1 ten 8 ones

Page 70
1. 20
2. 52
3. 65
4. 38
5. 78
6. 5 tens 9 ones
7. 2 tens 5 ones
8. 6 tens 1 one
9. 4 tens 0 ones
10. 3 tens 7 ones

Page 71
1. 18
2. 8
3. 17
4. 10
5. 14
6. 12
7. 18
8. 15
9. 14
10. 15
11. 20
12. 18
13. 20
14. 20
15. 19

Page 72
A. ones
B. tens
1. 27
2. 79
3. 36
4. 88
5. 48
6. 58
7. 19
8. 69
9. 99
10. 59

Page 73
1. 44
2. 89
3. 88
4. 99
5. 79
6. 99
7. 79
8. 99
9. 89
10. 97

Page 74
1. 8 tens – 80
2. 6 tens – 60
3. 6 tens – 60
4. 6 tens – 60
5. 9 tens – 90
6. 10 tens – 100
7. 7 tens – 70

Page 75
1. 4
2. 3
3. 4
4. 3
5. 3
6. 4
7. 4
8. 2

Page 76
1. 12
2. 21
3. 10
4. 10
5. 16
6. 47
7. 36
8. 67
9. 99
10. 76
11. 88
12. 99

Page 77
1. 7 – 2 = 5
2. 5 – 2 = 3
3. 3 – 2 = 1
4. 6 – 4 = 2
5. 8 – 3 = 5
6. 7 – 3 = 4

Page 78
1. 32
2. 51
3. 61
4. 50
5. 42
6. 26
7. 11
8. 73
9. 84
10. 22

Page 79
1. 17
2. 51
3. 3
4. 13
5. 24
6. 12
7. 20
8. 23
9. 7
10. 23
11. 21
12. 11
13. 16
14. 22
15. 12

Page 80
1. 15
2. 10
3. 2
4. 1
5. 6
6. 12
7. 13
8. 31
9. 11
10. 12
11. 1
12. 3
13. 5
14. 11
15. 11
16. 10
17. 32
18. 32
19. 3
20. 7

Page 81

1.
2.
3.
4.
5.
6.

Page 82
Automatic fill-in.

Page 83

1.
2.
3.
4.
5.
6.

Page 84
Automatic fill-in.

Page 85
1. 1/2
2. 1/4
3. 1/3
4. 1/3
5. 1/2
6. 1/4

Page 86
1. 2/4
2. 1/2
3. 2/3
4. 1/2
5. 2/3
6. 3/4

Page 87
1. 1/2
2. 1/4
3. 1/4
4. 1/3
5. 1/3
6. 1/2

Page 88
Automatic fill-in.

Page 89
Automatic fill-in.

Page 90
1. Tuesday
2. Saturday
3. Wednesday
4. Sunday

1. January
2. February
3. March
4. April
5. May
6. June
7. July
8. August
9. September
10. October
11. November
12. December

Page 91
1. 25°
2. 45°
3. 30°
4. 35°
5. 10°
6. 40°
7. 15°
8. 50°

Page 92
Varies

Page 93
2. 1¢
3. 25¢
4. 5¢
5. 10¢
6. 25¢
7. 25¢

Page 94

1. circle
2. rectangle
3. triangle

s	l	e	e	p
y	e	s	u	p
b	r	o	w	n
i	s	f	u	n
c	o	w	o	n

Circle the words in the puzzle.

Write the correct word in the blanks.

is	up
yes	fun
brown	cow
on	sleep

1. __ __ __, Amy may leave the room.
2. I want a red one, not a __ __ __ __ __ one.
3. Put the pan __ __ the stove.
4. It is night, and time to go to __ __ __ __ __.
5. What looks like a horse is really a __ __ __.
6. Please don't go __ __ the ladder.
7. Sandy __ __ only two years old.
8. Tom thinks school is __ __ __.

Circle the words in the puzzle.
Write the correct word in the blanks.

h	w	o	r	k
o	h	o	p	e
u	a	l	l	t
s	t	o	r	y
e	a	t	i	f

all   eat   hope   house

if   story   what   work

1. I __ __ __ __ you get to school on time.
2. Take __ __ __ of the cookies home with you.
3. It is time for Dad to go to __ __ __ __.
4. Be sure to __ __ __ all of your supper.
5. Juan lives in a red and white __ __ __ __ __.
6. Tom won't tell us __ __ he is going or not.
7. Our teacher read us a long __ __ __ __ __.
8. Amy did not know __ __   __ __ to say.

98

WHAT IS IT?

Use the first letter of each picture or the letter given to spell a new word.

bed   candy   coat   dear   eggs   glad   took   well

1. [bear] + e + [dog] = _ _ _

2. e + [gun] + [gun] + [star] = _ _ _ _

3. [car] + o + [apple] + [tree] = _ _ _ _

4. [wagon] + e + [leaf] + [leaf] = _ _ _ _

5. [drum] + [eye] + [airplane] + [ring] = _ _ _ _

6. [girl] + [lamp] + [apple] + [duck] = _ _ _ _

7. [cow] + [apple] + [nail] + [door] + [yarn] = _ _ _ _ _

8. [truck] + [owl] + [owl] + [kite] = _ _ _ _

Circle the words in the puzzle.

g	r	e	e	n
i	n	d	o	g
r	o	o	m	l
l	i	k	e	s
s	e	e	n	o

in
green
room
see
likes
no
dog
girls

Write the correct word in the blanks.

1. Brad put the baby kittens __ __ a box.
2. Sandy has a kitten, but not a __ __ __.
3. He __ __ __ __ __ to ride his bike.
4. The __ __ __ __ has blue walls.
5. The grass is __ __ __ __ __.
6. I don't __ __ __ the airplane in the sky, do you ?
7. __ __, you may not have a cookie.
8. They have five __ __ __ __ __ and no boys in their family.

100

Circle the words in the puzzle.

b	l	a	c	k
n	o	w	d	o
i	t	s	o	c
c	a	r	w	d
e	w	a	n	t

its	black
nice	car
now	do
want	down

Write the correct word in the blanks.

1. Go __ __ __ __ the stairs and turn right.
2. Please do the dishes __ __ __.
3. Bob is such a __ __ __ __ friend.
4. There is a __ __ __ __ __ spot on your dress.
5. The bird hurt __ __ __ wing.
6. I will show you how to __ __ it the right way.
7. Buckle your seat belt when you ride in the __ __ __.
8. My brothers __ __ __ __ a train set for Christmas.

Write the correct word in the blanks. Then write the word in the puzzle.

bring

girl

kitten

not

playing

think

when

yellow

ACROSS

1. A banana is a __ __ __ __ __ __ fruit.
2. __ __ __ __ __ before you give your answer.
3. Judy is a __ __ __ __.

DOWN

1. Tommy is __ __ __ __ __ __ __ outside today.
2. Father does __ __ __ know what time it is.
3. Sue doesn't know __ __ __ __ they are leaving on vacation.
4. Please __ __ __ __ __ your books when you come.
5. A __ __ __ __ __ __ will grow up to be a cat.

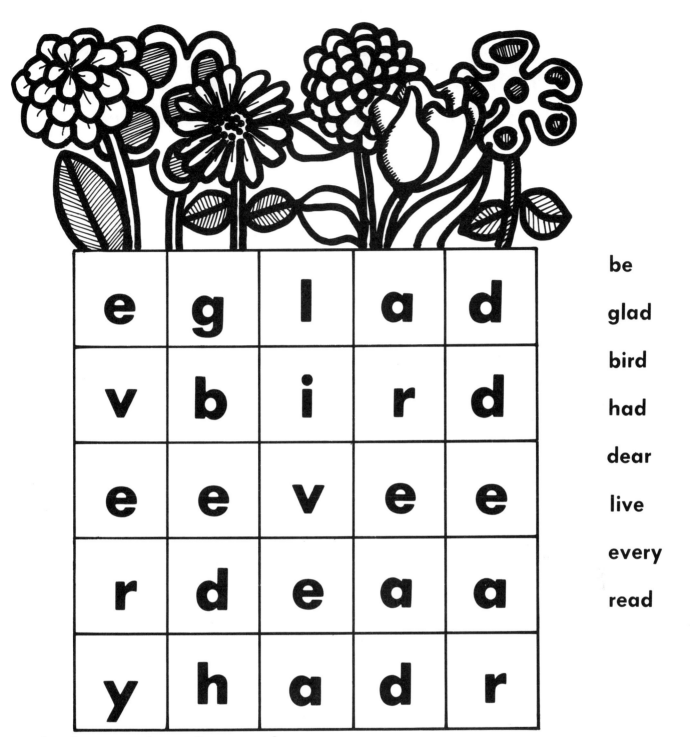

e	g	l	a	d
v	b	i	r	d
e	e	v	e	e
r	d	e	a	a
y	h	a	d	r

be

glad

bird

had

dear

live

every

read

Circle the words in the puzzle.
Write the correct word in the blanks.

1. That __ __ __ __ goes south for the winter.
2. I do not want to __ __ in your way.
3. I am __ __ __ __ to hear that you can come.
4. We can begin a letter by saying, "__ __ __ __ Sir."
5. __ __ __ __ __ child will go to this party.
6. Where does the new girl __ __ __ __?
7. Sue will __ __ __ __ the book to her brother.
8. I __ __ __ a penny, but I lost it.

MISSING VOWELS

Fill in the missing vowels (A,E,I,O and U) for these members of a family.

1. m __ th __ r
2. k __ tt __ n
3. __ __ nt
4. s __ st __ r
5. f __ th __ r
6. d __ g
7. gr __ ndm __
8. gr __ ndp __
9. br __ th __ r
10. __ ncl __

Circle the words in the puzzle. Write the correct word in the blanks.

f	o	u	r	h
r	w	i	l	l
o	h	i	m	i
m	a	n	y	k
I	s	m	a	e

four   from   has   him

I   like   many   will

1. How __ __ __ __ people came to the show?
2. __ will stay with you all the time.
3. Sandy is __ __ __ __ feet tall.
4. Gina __ __ __ __ be the first girl to win.
5. He says he doesn't __ __ __ __ peas.
6. My friend __ __ __ a pet snake.
7. Be sure to let __ __ __ have a turn.
8. Juan is __ __ __ __ the country of Mexico.

**Write the correct word in the blanks.
Then write the word in the puzzle.**

for   look   father

letter   pet   bear

first   pretty

ACROSS

1. My brother thinks she is a very __ __ __ __ __ __ girl.
2. I wish the mailman would leave me a __ __ __ __ __ __.
3. That present is __ __ __ Jim.
4. My baby brother said his __ __ __ __ __ word today.

DOWN

1. My dog Spot is my __ __ __.
2. Before you cross the street, stop, __ __ __ __, and listen.
3. The man driving the car is my __ __ __ __ __ __.
4. They say there is a big __ __ __ __ in these woods.

106

g	h	e	l	p
r	a	t	m	b
a	o	o	i	e
d	f	y	l	s
e	f	s	k	t

best
grade
help
milk
off
rat
toys

Circle the words in the puzzle.

Write the correct word in the blanks.

1. Mrs. Van teaches second __ __ __ __ __ in our school.
2. A __ __ __ looks very much like a large mouse.
3. Be sure to put your __ __ __ __ away before going to bed.
4. If you can't do the work alone, ask for __ __ __ __.
5. The __ __ __ __ you drink comes from cows.
6. Please turn __ __ __ the light.
7. Amy is the __ __ __ __ ball player in our whole class.

**Write the correct word in the blanks.
Then write the word in the puzzle.**

apples   did   found   you

boys   tell   old   put

ACROSS

1. My mother uses ＿ ＿ ＿ ＿ ＿ ＿ to make my favorite pie.
2. Your teacher wants to see ＿ ＿ ＿.
3. My grandmother is very ＿ ＿ ＿.
4. Yes, I ＿ ＿ ＿ enjoy my trip.

DOWN

1. Please, ＿ ＿ ＿ your books away.
2. Andy said he wouldn't ＿ ＿ ＿ ＿ my mother.
3. There are more ＿ ＿ ＿ ＿ than girls in our class.
4. The lost and ＿ ＿ ＿ ＿ ＿ box is in the office.

Circle the words in the puzzle.

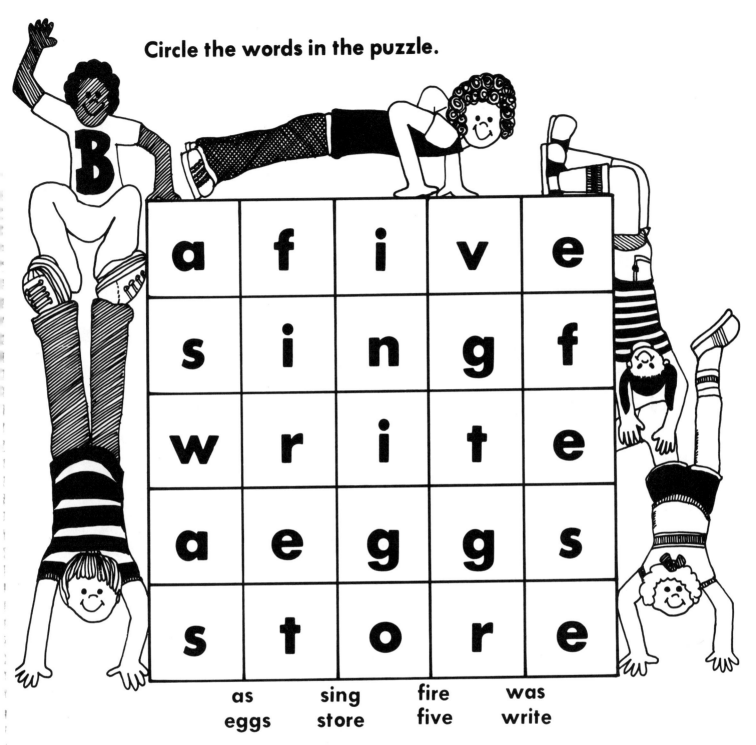

a	f	i	v	e
s	i	n	g	f
w	r	i	t	e
a	e	g	g	s
s	t	o	r	e

as	sing	fire	was
eggs	store	five	write

Write the correct word in the blanks.

1. She wants someone to _ _ _ _ _ her a letter.
2. Tom had four and he wanted _ _ _ _.
3. Mom went to the _ _ _ _ _ for cheese.
4. That bell means there is a _ _ _ _ .
5. He loves to _ _ _ _ that song.
6. Daddy likes _ _ _ _ for breakfast.
7. Grandma _ _ _ sad, but now she is happy.
8. Kim is _ _ tall as I am.

come
dogs
get
made
much
one
school
some

**Write the correct word in the blanks.
Then write the word in the puzzle.**

ACROSS

1. Dad ate too __ __ __ __ for Thanksgiving.
2. We hope Amy will __ __ __ __ to the party.
3. Our baby isn't even __ __ __ year old.
4. I heard a lot of __ __ __ __ barking last night.

DOWN

1. I will take __ __ __ __ of the apples home with me.
2. My sister will go to __ __ __ __ __ __ this year.
3. Sandy __ __ __ __ the dress herself.
4. Do you know what you are going to __ __ __ for Christmas?

110

a	f	t	e	r
t	r	e	e	t
e	y	e	s	a
g	o	t	a	s
d	a	y	w	e

after
ate
day
eyes
got
saw
tree
we

Circle the words in the puzzle.   Write the correct word in the blanks.

1. We are going out to eat __ __ __ __ __ the game.
2. I __ __ __ you run into the house.
3. __ __ will all sing together.
4. Sandy __ __ __ four presents for her birthday.
5. The cat ran up the __ __ __ __ .
6. Karen has brown hair and blue __ __ __ __ .
7. It is a nice __ __ __ for a walk.
8. Grandpa __ __ __ too much for lunch.

an   bed   candy   jump

red   sled   tricks   your

ACROSS

1. Let's teach your dog to do some __ __ __ __ __ __.
2. Too much __ __ __ __ __ is bad for your teeth.
3. My dad is out of __ __ __ very early every morning.
4. Don't __ __ __ __ off the roof! You'll get hurt!

DOWN

1. I would like __ __ egg for breakfast.
2. Jane likes her __ __ __ shorts the best.
3. Is that __ __ __ __ new skateboard?
4. My dog can pull our __ __ __ __ in the snow.

WATCH OUT FOR THE HILL!

c	a	m	e	f
f	i	s	h	g
o	b	h	e	i
o	i	s	o	v
d	g	a	v	e

big   so

came   gave

fish   he

give   food

1. We catch __ __ __ __ in the lake.
2. Tom will __ __ __ __ me a turn next.
3. We eat good __ __ __ __ to stay healthy.
4. Grandma __ __ __ __ to our house on Sunday.
5. She didn't sleep, but __ __ did.
6. I __ __ __ __ Bill a chance to try it.
7. We're late, __ __ hurry up and get dressed.
8. We have a very __ __ __ dog.

113

YES AND NO

Find the word which means exactly the opposite of the word given.
The first one is done for you.

asleep   sit
lost   skinny
she   small
short   stop
sister   yours

1. he   s h e

2. tall   s __ __ __ __

3. brother   __ __ s __ __ __

4. start   s __ __ __

5. mine   __ __ __ __ s

6. fat   s __ __ __ __ __

7. stand   s __ __

8. awake   __ s __ __ __ __

9. found   __ __ s __

10. big   s __ __ __ __

d	w	i	s	h
r	u	n	h	m
e	t	h	e	a
s	n	o	w	k
s	g	a	m	e

dress   she

game   snow

make   the

run   wish

1. He likes it when she wears her red __ __ __ __ __.
2. Everybody likes __ __ __ __ on Christmas day.
3. Tell Jane __ __ __ may use my skateboard.
4. My grandpa likes to __ __ __ __ things out of wood.
5. We __ __ __ __ you were here with us.
6. Our dog tries to __ __ __ as fast as our car.
7. We are going to the baseball __ __ __ __.
8. He is __ __ __ tallest boy in our class.

Write the correct word in the blanks. Then write the word in the puzzle.

baby
blue
boat
our
play
please
then
wagon

ACROSS

1. Always say __ __ __ __ __ __ and thank-you.
2. My brother is still a __ __ __ __.
3. That red car belongs to __ __ __ family.
4. First we wash, __ __ __ __ we eat.

DOWN

1. When it's raining, you can't __ __ __ __ outside.
2. Kathy went to the lake for a __ __ __ __ ride.
3. My favorite color is __ __ __ __.
4. Molly has a new red __ __ __ __ __.

116

Circle the words in the puzzle.
Write the correct word in the blanks.

a	b	o	u	t
m	a	y	t	a
b	l	u	s	k
e	l	o	v	e
p	a	r	t	y

about	am	ball	love
may	party	take	us

1. I am going to a birthday __ __ __ __ __.
2. Her mother said she __ __ __ go to the beach.
3. I __ __ going to run to the corner.
4. The story is __ __ __ __ __ Jody and her cat.
5. The valentine said, "I __ __ __ __ You."
6. Please __ __ __ __ the dog for a walk.
7. Throw the __ __ __ __ to second base.
8. Those boys want to ride their bikes with __ __.

ACROSS

1. Larry is going fishing ___ ___ ___ ___ his dad.
2. He ___ ___ ___ ___ my truck, but he gave it back.
3. Linda likes to ride her ___ ___ ___ ___ ___.
4. Part of a minute is a ___ ___ ___ ___ ___ ___.

DOWN

1. I would like a drink of ___ ___ ___ ___ ___ , please.
2. Wait, I want a ride, ___ ___ ___!
3. Our teacher ___ ___ ___ in a race.
4. Roberto thinks he ___ ___ ___ fix his boat.

118

THE FUNNY WOODS

My mother laughs when I tell her that there are funny things hiding in the woods behind our house. But you and I know better, don't we? Fill in the answer for the clues given, and then circle the "funny thing" in its hiding place.

boots   **fish**   **fork**   **hat**

mouse   **pony**   **train**   **watch**

1. I always wear a __ __ __ on my head in cold weather.
2. A small horse is called a __ __ __ __.
3. A __ __ __ __ __ has an engine, box cars, and a caboose.
4. Use worms when you go to the lake to catch __ __ __ __.
5. Wear __ __ __ __ __ over your shoes when it snows.
6. By my __ __ __ __ __, it's time to leave.
7. Use your __ __ __ __, not your spoon, to eat your meat.
8. A __ __ __ __ __ likes to eat cheese.

119

little   their
out   very
over   well
said   would

ACROSS

1. I __ __ __ __ __ like to go along, but I have to stay here.
2. Sally is too __ __ __ __ __ __ to reach the sink.
3. You should be __ __ __ __ happy today.
4. Bob __ __ __ __ he wouldn't be ready on time.

DOWN

1. Some people get water out of a __ __ __ __ __.
2. The dog ran __ __ __ the door.
3. On our trip we flew __ __ __ __ the ocean.
4. That ball belongs to __ __ __ __ __ school.

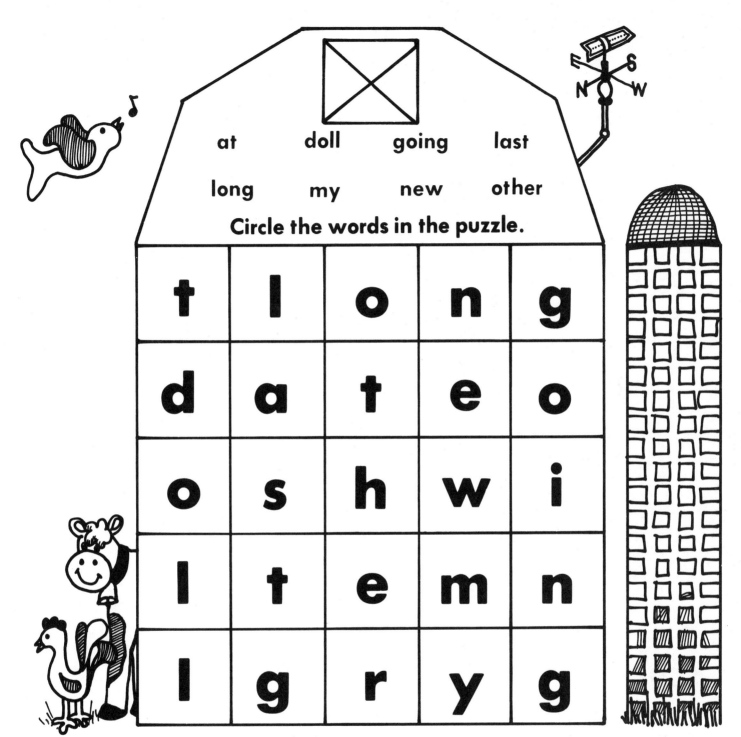

at doll going last

long my new other

Circle the words in the puzzle.

t	l	o	n	g
d	a	t	e	o
o	s	h	w	i
l	t	e	m	n
l	g	r	y	g

Write the correct word in the blanks.

1. Ed is not _ _ _ _ _ with us today.
2. My sister takes her _ _ _ _ to bed.
3. These pants are too _ _ _ _ for me.
4. What _ _ _ _ _ colors do you have?
5. Tony is _ _ his mother's office.
6. Mr. Andrews is _ _ gym teacher.
7. We need a _ _ _ car.
8. Larry said he would go _ _ _ _ instead of first.

Write the correct word in the blanks.
Then write the word in the puzzle.

back

cold

book

have

by

her

coat

here

ACROSS

1. It is windy and __ __ __ __ out today.
2. Dad will be __ __ __ __ in an hour.
3. My cousins __ __ __ __ six cows in their barn.
4. Jenny says that lady is __ __ __ aunt.

DOWN

1. Grandma is reading a new __ __ __ __.
2. Joan is sitting __ __ the door.
3. I wear a __ __ __ __ when it's cold.
4. Come! You can see the mountains from __ __ __ __.

122

LET'S TAKE A TRIP

These are things we pack for a trip. What are they?

apple   map

balls   shoes

coat   socks

hat   toothbrush

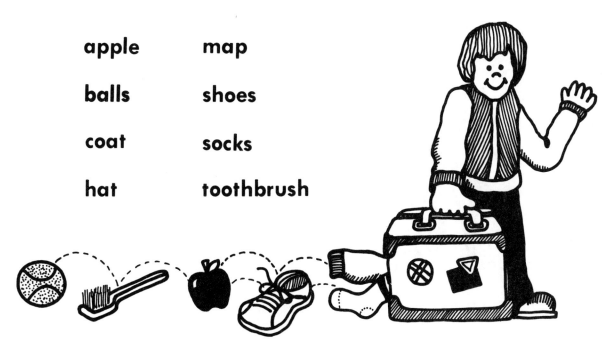

1. You'll need this to keep your teeth clean.
   __ oo __ __ __ __ u __ __

2. You'll wear it to keep your head warm.
   __ a __

3. This __ a __ will help us find our way.

4. You wear them on your feet.
   __ __oe __ and __ o __ __ __

5. I'll need my __ o a __ for cold days.

6. I almost forgot to bring tennis __ a __ __ __ .

7. This a __ __ __ e will keep me from getting hungry.

Write the correct word in the blanks.   Then write the word in the puzzle.

birds   rabbit   man   mother

his   sister   three   went

ACROSS

1. My dad saw a __ __ __ __ __ __ hop across our yard.
2. That lady over there is my __ __ __ __ __ __.
3. Pedro got hurt and __ __ __ __ home.
4. I have a new baby __ __ __ __ __ __!

DOWN

1. Jon lost __ __ __ bike.
2. My dad is a tall __ __ __.
3. Not all __ __ __ __ __ can fly.
4. Amy is only __ __ __ __ __ years old.

124

Write the correct word in the blanks.
Then write the word in the puzzle.

go
good
how
morning
soon
them
things
were

ACROSS

1. I don't know __ __ __ to do it.
2. Be sure to eat a good breakfast in the __ __ __ __ __ __ __.
3. Amy wants to __ __ along.
4. We will be leaving for Grandma's house very __ __ __ __.

DOWN

1. I do not want to go with __ __ __ __.
2. How many of your friends __ __ __ __ at the party?
3. Come get your __ __ __ __ __ __ for the trip.
4. My mother makes very __ __ __ __ cookies.

SILLY FARM

Help the animals get to the barn on this Silly Farm. Write the letters in the blanks. The last letter of one word is the first letter of the next word.

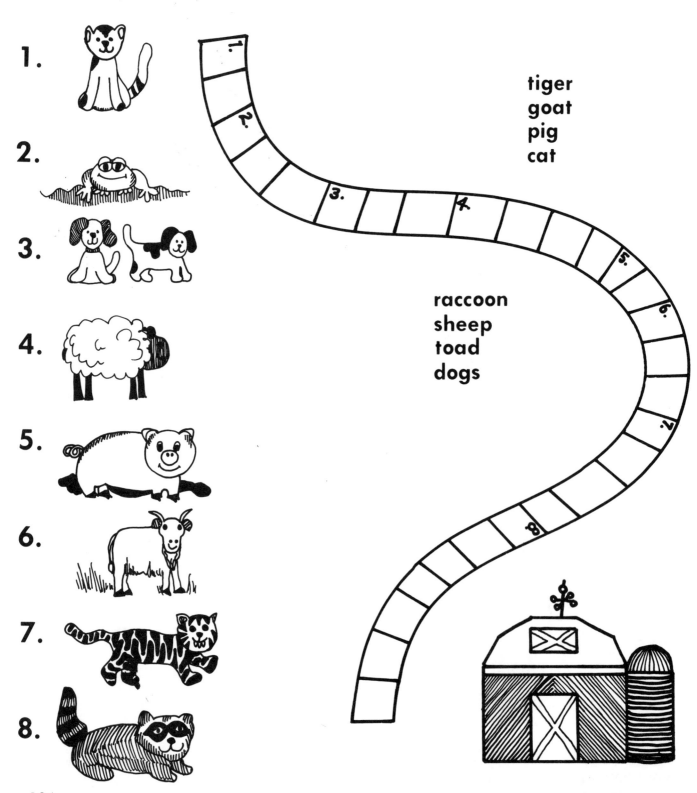

1.

2.

3.

4.

5.

6.

7.

8.

tiger
goat
pig
cat

raccoon
sheep
toad
dogs

Page 97
1. yes
2. brown
3. on
4. sleep
5. cow
6. up
7. is
8. fun

Page 98
1. hope
2. all
3. work
4. eat
5. house
6. if
7. story
8. what

Page 99
1. bed
2. eggs
3. coat
4. well
5. dear
6. glad
7. candy
8. took

Page 100
1. in
2. dog
3. likes
4. room
5. green
6. see
7. No
8. girls

Page 101
1. down
2. now
3. nice
4. black
5. its
6. do
7. car
8. want

Page 102
Across
1. yellow
2. think
3. girl

Down
1. playing
2. not
3. when
4. bring
5. kitten

Page 103
1. bird
2. be
3. glad
4. Dear
5. Every
6. live
7. read
8. had

Page 104
1. mother
2. kitten
3. aunt
4. sister
5. father
6. dog
7. grandma
8. grandpa
9. brother
10. uncle

Page 105
1. many
2. I
3. four
4. will
5. like
6. has
7. him
8. from

Page 106
Across
1. pretty
2. letter
3. for
4. first

Down
1. pet
2. look
3. father
4. bear

Page 107
1. grade
2. rat
3. toys
4. help
5. milk
6. off
7. best

Page 108
Across
1. apples
2. you
3. old
4. did

Down
1. put
2. tell
3. boys
4. found

Page 109
1. write
2. five
3. store
4. fire
5. sing
6. eggs
7. was
8. as

Page 110
Across
1. much
2. come
3. one
4. dogs

Down
1. some
2. school
3. made
4. get

Page 111
1. after
2. saw
3. We
4. got
5. tree
6. eyes
7. day
8. ate

Page 112
Across
1. tricks
2. candy
3. bed
4. jump

Down
1. an
2. red
3. your
4. sled

Page 113
1. fish
2. give
3. food
4. came
5. he
6. gave
7. so
8. big

Page 114
1. she
2. short
3. sister
4. stop
5. yours
6. skinny
7. sit
8. asleep
9. lost
10. small

Page 115
1. dress
2. snow
3. she
4. make
5. wish
6. run
7. game
8. the

Page 116
Across
1. please
2. baby
3. our
4. then

Down
1. play
2. boat
3. blue
4. wagon

Page 117
1. party
2. may
3. am
4. about
5. Love
6. take
7. ball
8. us

Page 118
Across
1. with
2. took
3. horse
4. second

Down
1. water
2. too
3. ran
4. can

Page 119
1. hat
2. pony
3. train
4. fish
5. boots
6. watch
7. fork
8. mouse

Page 120
Across
1. would
2. little
3. very
4. said

Down
1. well
2. out
3. over
4. their

Page 121
1. going
2. doll
3. long
4. other
5. at
6. my
7. new
8. last

Page 122
Across
1. cold
2. back
3. have
4. her

Down
1. book
2. by
3. coat
4. here

Page 123
1. toothbrush
2. hat
3. map
4. shoes – socks
5. coat
6. balls
7. apple

Page 124
Across
1. rabbit
2. mother
3. went
4. sister

Down
1. his
2. man
3. birds
4. three

Page 125
Across
1. how
2. morning
3. go
4. soon

Down
1. them
2. were
3. things
4. good

Page 126
1. cat
2. toad
3. dogs
4. sheep
5. pig
6. goat
7. tiger
8. raccoon

bl

BL stands for the Blue Blender! He puts letters together and makes the sounds of the letters glide together.

Help the Blue Blender make the words below. Add the right letters to make a word and answer the riddle. Then color the Blue Blender. Color his suit blue!

The color of the sky.   __ __ ue

You play with these.   __ __ ocks

The color of the night.   __ __ ack

You do this to birthday candles.   __ __ ow

cl

Cl stands for Clara Clown.
Color all the words that start with cl.

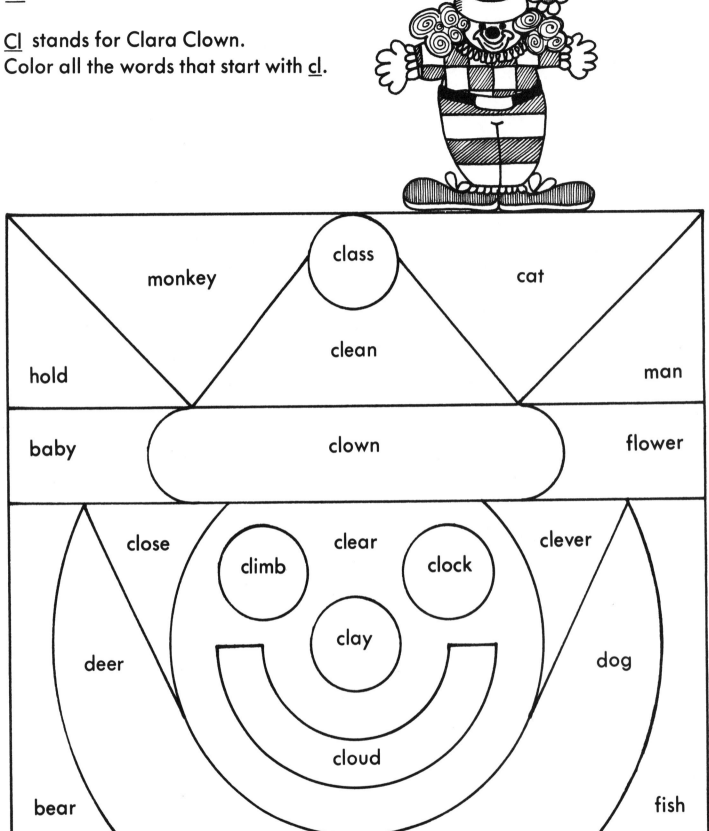

monkey

class

cat

clean

hold

man

baby

clown

flower

close

clear

clever

climb

clock

clay

deer

dog

cloud

bear

fish

The picture is of a _ _ _ _ _.

fl

Fl stands for Flora Flower.
Add fl to the words. Then draw a line from the word to the picture.

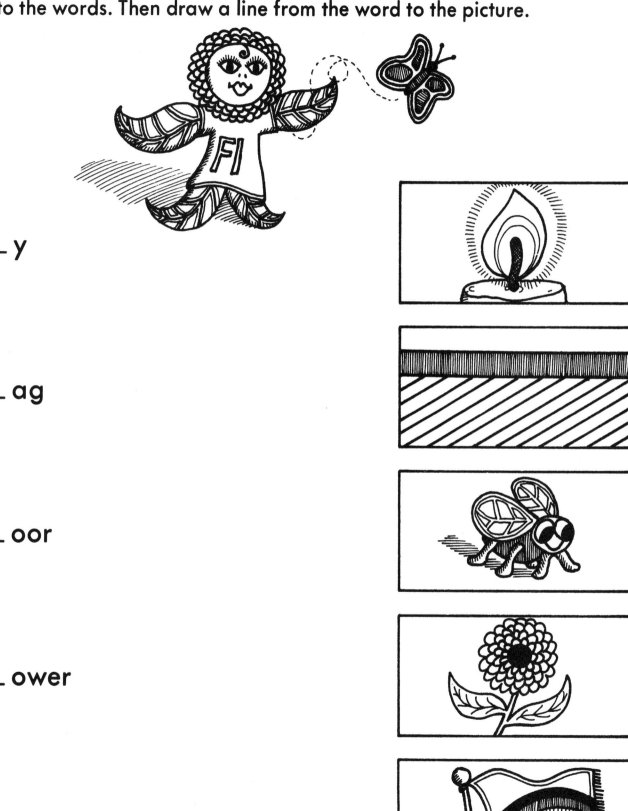

___ ___ y

___ ___ ag

___ ___ oor

___ ___ ower

___ ___ ame

gl

Gl stands for Glad Gloria!

Wait! Glad Gloria is not glad! She is sad! She is sad because she has lost three things. They all begin with gl. Help her find the things. Draw a line around them. Then write the words below.

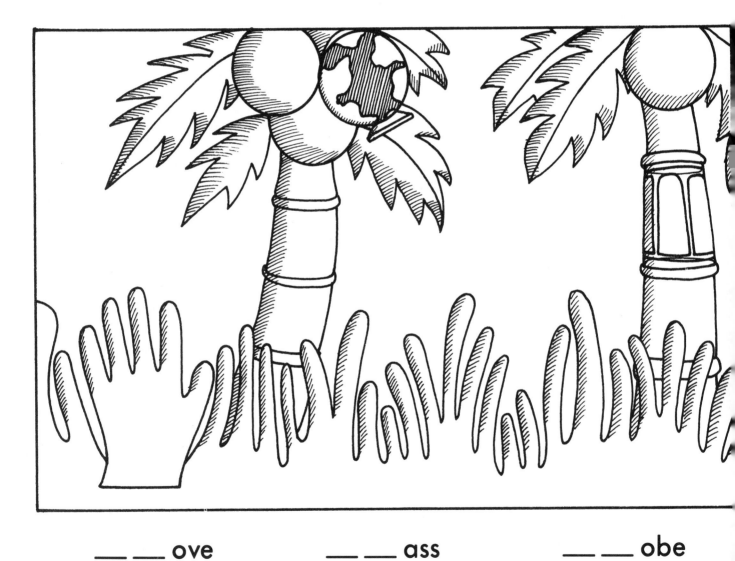

___ ___ ove   ___ ___ ass   ___ ___ obe

How will Gloria feel when she finds the things she lost? ___ ___ ___ ___

132

pl

PI stands for please.

Circle the word that begins with pl.

1. pet   gold   plan

2. play   snake   blue

3. green   chair   plant

4. book   place   dark

5. please   clown   parade

sl

<u>Sl</u> stands for Sleepy Slim.

Draw a line around the pictures that begin with the <u>sl</u> sound.

134

REVIEW: l blends

Are you handy with blends? Let's see if you are. Write each blend once to make a new word. Say the new word.

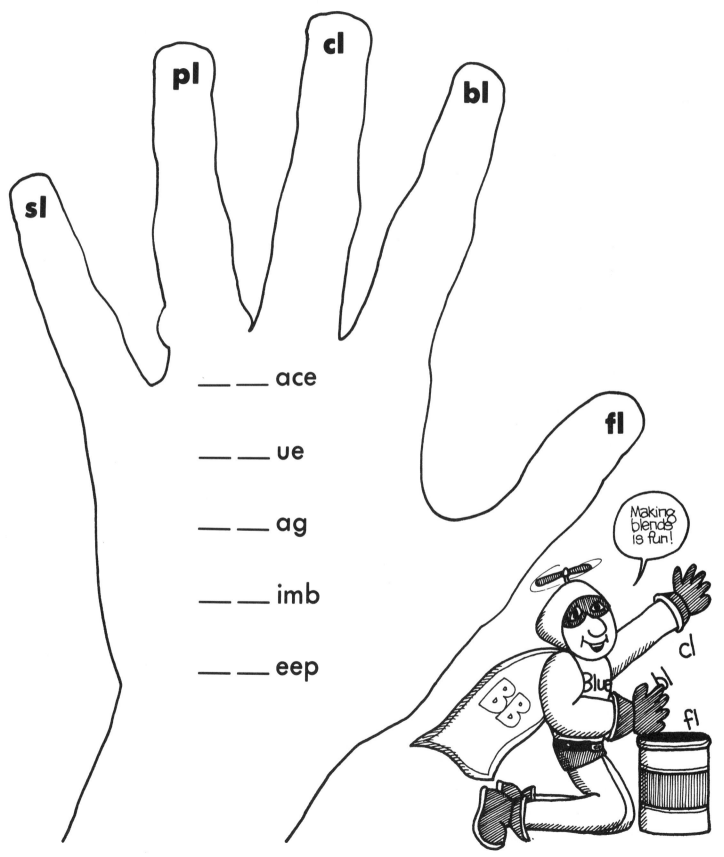

sl pl cl bl fl

___ ___ ace

___ ___ ue

___ ___ ag

___ ___ imb

___ ___ eep

Making blends is fun!

br

Br stands for branches.

Write the correct word on each branch. Say the word.

2. My _____ is six today.

3. We had to go over a _____.

1. I need a _____ and dust pan.

4. The sun was _____.

5. The man was _____.

6. The _____ fell from the tree.

branch

brave

bright

brook

broom

brother

My brother brags that he is brave.

cr

Cr stands for Crazy Crow.

Draw a line around six picture words that begin with cr.

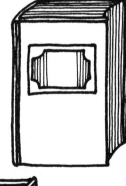

137

dr

Dr stands for drivers!

Color the dr words green.

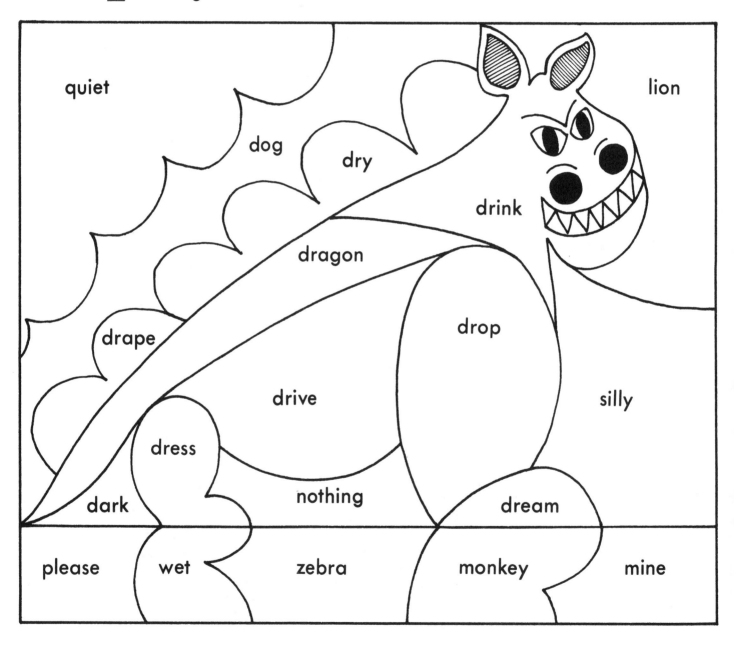

quiet

lion

dog

dry

drink

dragon

drape

drop

drive

silly

dress

dark

nothing

dream

please wet zebra monkey mine

This is a picture of a (dress dragon driver).

138

fr

<u>Fr</u> stands for Friendly Frog.

Friendly Frog likes to ask riddles. Read his riddles. Then write the answers.

| frog | from | friend | front | fruits | frighten |

1. Somebody you like is a _____.

2. It is not the back. It is the _____.

3. Suzie got a present _____ Jimmy.

4. A green animal that hops is a _____.

5. Apples, oranges, and bananas are _____.

6. If you scare somebody, you _____ them.

Here, Friendly Frog. Have some fresh fruit!

gr

Gr stands for green grass. Color the grass green.

Add gr to each word. Say the word.

1. __ __ een

2. __ __ ass

3. __ __ andmother

4. __ __ apes

5. __ __ asshopper

6. __ __ ill

7. __ __ andfather

140

pr

Pr stands for Proud Prince.

Connect the dots.
You will see what the Proud Prince is holding.

He is holding a (frog pretty present).

Draw a line around seven words that start with pr.

pretty

peanut

night

present

day

princess

prize

girl

pray

black

turtle

proud

prison

tr

Tr stands for train.

Draw a line around the blend that begins each picture word.

bl ... pr	tr ... br	cl ... cr
tr ... pl	gl ... gr	bl ... tr
tr ... br	cl ... tr	fr ... pl
gr ... pr	fr ... br	pr ... tr

Trudy tried a trick. She trapped a train.

142

REVIEW: r blends

Help the train go down the track. Make a word at each stop.
Use one of the blends to make a word.

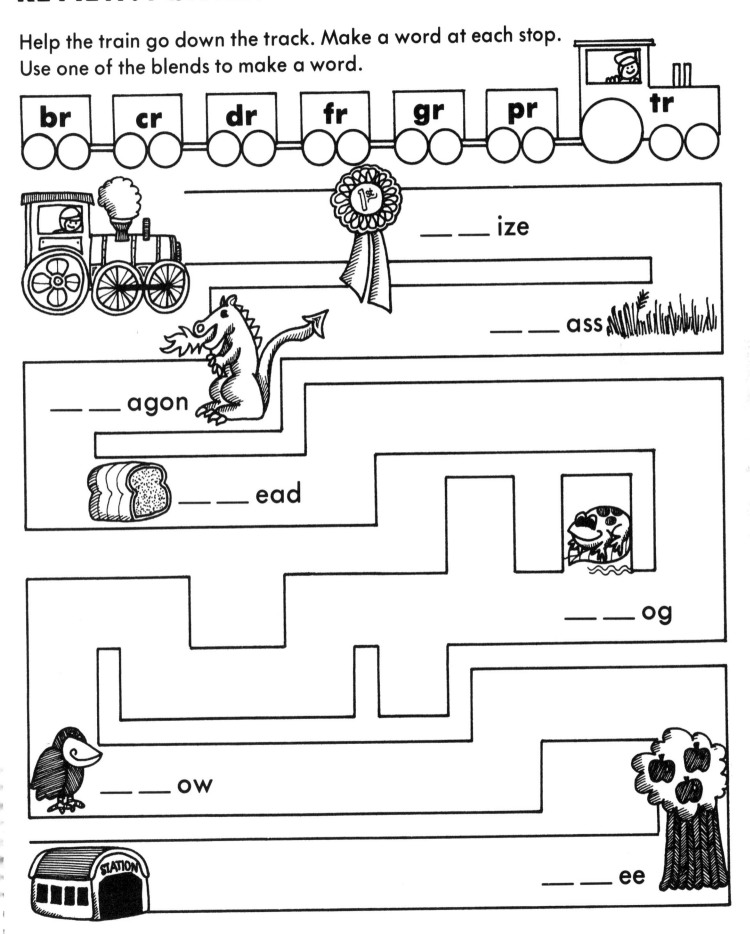

br **cr** **dr** **fr** **gr** **pr** **tr**

___ ___ ize

___ ___ ass

___ ___ agon

___ ___ ead

___ ___ og

___ ___ ow

___ ___ ee

143

sw

Sw is for swim.

sp

Sp is for Spot.

Make a word. Put the right letters in front of the word.
Say the word. Draw a line from the word to the picture.

__ __ ider

__ __ im

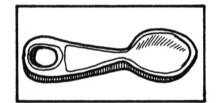

__ __ oon

__ __ an

Write two words that begin with sw.   Write two words that begin with sp.

_____   _____

_____   _____

sm

Sm is for small.

sn

Sn is for snail.

Draw a line around the picture that starts with the blend in the box.

sm			
sn			
sn			
sm			
sm			
sn			

Smart snails always smile at snakes!

st

St is for Start and Stop!

Start and Stop are lost! Help them get home. Draw a line from
Start and Stop to the next st word. Then to the next. If you follow
the st words, Start and Stop will get home.

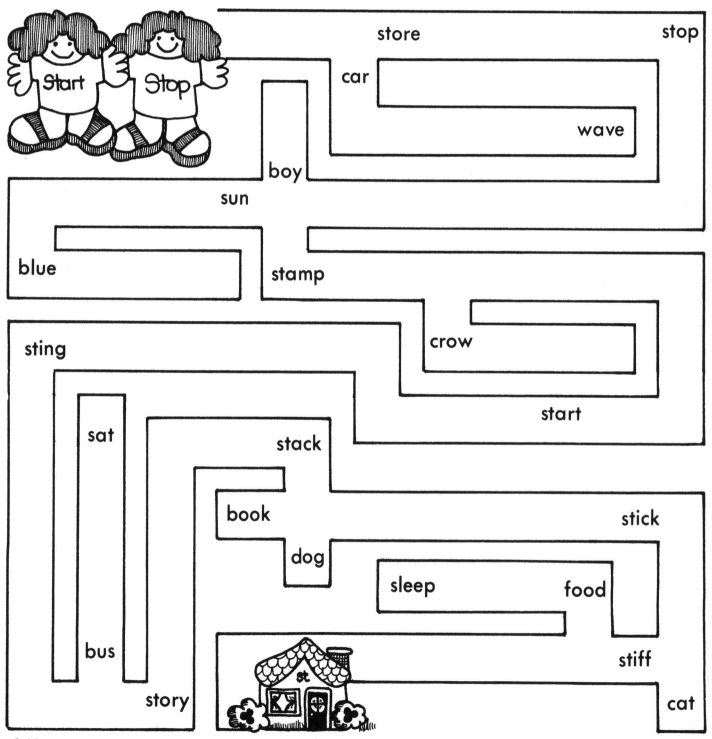

store

stop

car

wave

boy

sun

blue

stamp

crow

sting

start

sat

stack

book

stick

dog

sleep

food

bus

stiff

story

cat

146

st

<u>St</u> can also end words. Then it stands for last.
It is the last sound in last!

Color the words that end in <u>st</u> red.

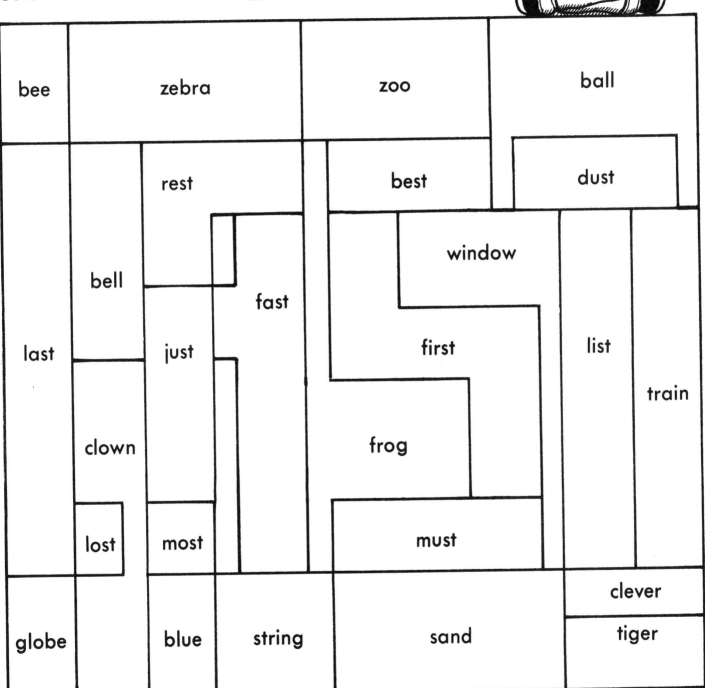

The picture says __ __ __ __.

str

Str is for string.

spr

Spr is for spring.

Draw a line around the picture that starts with the blend given.

spr	
str	
str	
str	
str	

REVIEW: s blends

Look at the picture. Say the picture word. Draw a line around the beginning blend. Write the blend on the blanks. Say the word.

str  **sl**	**sl**  **sn**	**sm**  **st**
__ __ __ awberry	__ __ ail	__ __ amp
sp  **str**	**st** 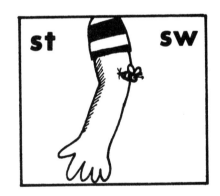 **sw**	**st**  **sm**
__ __ __ ing	__ __ ing	__ __ ile
sw  **sl**	**sl**  **st**	**spr** 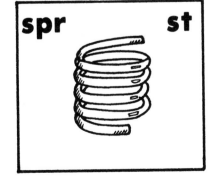 **st**
__ __ im	__ __ op	__ __ __ ing

149

ch

Ch is for cheese.

Circle the picture that <u>begins</u> with the <u>ch</u> sound.

Ch is also for porch.

Circle the picture that <u>ends</u> with the <u>ch</u> sound.

ch

ch

ch

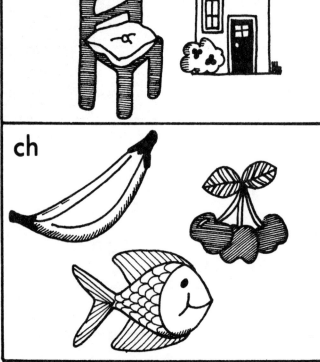

ch

ch

150

sh

Sh is for sheep.   Sh is also for fish.

Sheep and Fish are all mixed up. They don't know which word belongs to them. Put all the words that start with <u>sh</u> in the sheep pen. Put all the words that end with <u>sh</u> in the fish pond.

ship	shell	dish	shoe	wish
show	shop	wash	shirt	push

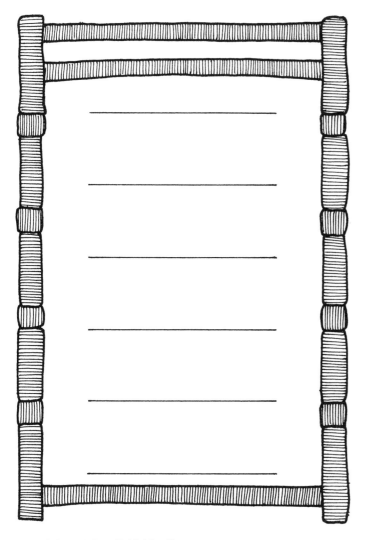

th

Th is for thumb.    Th is also for mouth.

Here are some riddles. Put the correct word on the line to answer the riddle.

bath	south	thing	path	thank	think

1. "_____ you, Grandma," said Jeff.

2. Karen did not want to take a _____.

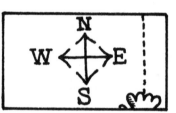

3. Birds fly _____ for the winter.

4. I _____ I know the answer.

5. What is this _____?

6. The _____ went into the woods.

wh

Wh is for whale.

Draw a line around the words or the pictures that begin with wh.

wh			
wh	wagon	vase	wheat
wh			
wh	man	woman	why
wh			
wh	green	white	yellow

DIGRAPH REVIEW: <u>ch</u>, <u>sh</u>, <u>th</u>, <u>wh</u>

Draw a line from the letters to the picture words that begin or end with them.

REVIEW

Match the socks to make words. Draw a line from each beginning
sock to each ending sock.

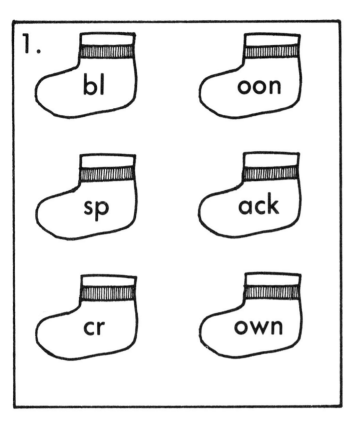

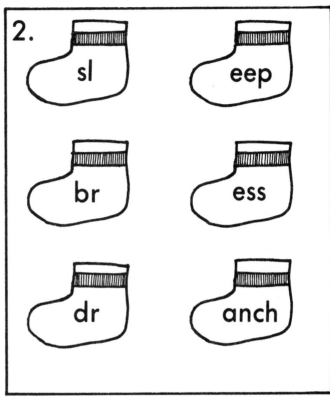

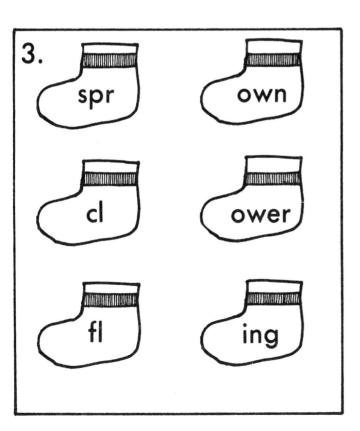

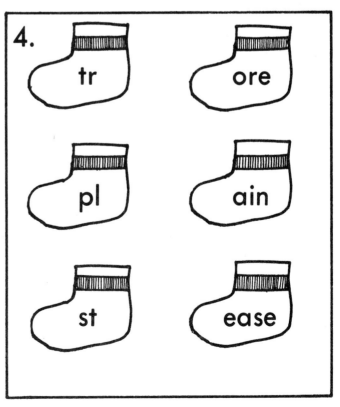

REVIEW

Help the Blue Blender. Make a word for each blend. Write it on the line.

_____   _____

_____   _____

_____   _____

_____   _____

_____   _____

DIGRAPHS REVIEW: <u>ch</u>, <u>sh</u>, <u>th</u>, <u>wh</u>

Draw a line from the letters to the picture words that begin with them.

REVIEW

Be a worker in the word factory! Make four words in each row. Add the right blend to the last three letters to make a word. Write each word on the line.

| bl | br | cl | cr | dr | sl | sm | sn | st | tr |

own   **ack**   **ick**

_____   _____   _____

_____   _____   _____

_____   _____   _____

_____   _____   _____

REVIEW

Never forget your friend, Blue Blender!

Read each sentence. Circle the word that starts with the blend given.

pl   1. The girl looked up at the plane.

sn   2. The snail won the race!

pr   3. The prize was a gold cup.

sp   4. Spot had a stick in his mouth.

dr   5. The man drank the water.

gl   6. He drank it from a glass.

sw   7. The cookie was too sweet.

Page 129
Automatic
fill-in.

Page 130
class	clock
clean	close
clown	clever
clear	cloud
clay	(clown)
climb	

Page 131
Automatic
fill-in.

Page 132
Automatic
fill-in. (glad)

Page 133
1. plan
2. play
3. plant
4. place
5. please

Page 134
sleep
sled
slide
Sleepy Slim

Page 135
1. place
2. blue
3. flag
4. climb
5. sleep

Page 136
1. broom
2. brother
3. brook
4. bright
5. brave
6. branch

Page 137
crown
crow
cross
crib
crayon
cry

Page 138
dress
drop
dragon
drape
dream
drink
dry
drive
(dragon)

Page 139
1. friend
2. front
3. from
4. frog
5. fruits
6. frighten

Page 140
Automatic
fill-in.

Page 141
(present)
pretty
prize
proud
prison
princess
pray
present

Page 142
All begin
with tr.

Page 143
prize
grass
dragon
bread
frog
crow
tree

Page 144
spider
swim
spoon
swan

Page 145
smoke
snowman
snail
smell
smile
snake

Page 146
store
stop
stamp
start
sting
story
stack
stick
stiff

Page 147
last	list
rest	most
just	best
lost	first
fast	must
dust	(last)

Page 148
sprinkler
spring
strawberry
stream
string

Page 149
str sn st
str st sm
sw st spr

Page 150
church
chair
cherries
porch
match
watch

Page 151
ship	dish
shell	wish
shoe	wash
show	push
shop	
shirt	

Page 152
1. thank
2. bath
3. south
4. think
5. thing
6. path

Page 153
wheel
wheat
whistle
why
whale
white

Page 154
ch	th
match	teeth
chair	or mouth
chicken	thumb
sh	path
sheep	wh
shell	wheel
dish	whale

Page 155
black	sleep
spoon	branch
crown	dress
spring	train
clown	please
flower	store

Page 156
Any combination
drag, drink, drove
free, frog
crib, crock
flag, flee, flock
true, trot, tree
snag, snowman
clue, clog, clot, clock
glue, glee, glove
blot, block, blink, blue
spot

Page 157
ch	th
chicken	thumb
church	thirty
sh	wh
shoe	whale
ship	wheel

Page 158
own	ack	ick
blown	black	brick
brown	clack	click
clown	crack	slick
crown	slack	stick
drown	smack	trick
	snack	
	stack	
	track	

Page 159
1. plane
2. snail
3. prize
4. spot
5. drank
6. glass
7. sweet

BEGINNING CONSONANTS

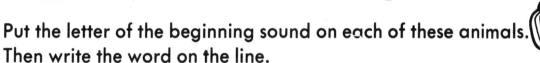

Put the letter of the beginning sound on each of these animals.
Then write the word on the line.

__ightingale _____

__ear _____

__ig _____

__at _____

__uail _____

__og _____

__abbit _____

__ish _____

__eal _____

__oat _____

__iger _____

__orse _____

__ulture _____

__aguar _____

__alrus _____

__angaroo_____

fo__ _____

__ion _____

__ak _____

__ouse_____

__ebra_____

SHORT "A" WORDS

Read the short "a" words in the apple.
Then do what each sentence tells you.

at   as
cat fan am
ant an   had

1. Write the spelling words that have two letters.

_____ _____ _____ _____

2. Write the spelling words that have three letters.

_____ _____ _____ _____

Make new words. Trace over the beginning letter.
Write the short "a" family after it. Now say the word.

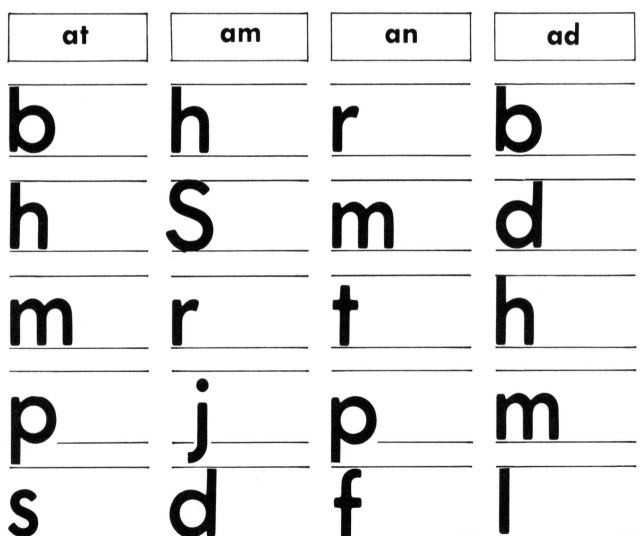

at	am	an	ad
b	h	r	b
h	S	m	d
m	r	t	h
p	j	p	m
s	d	f	l

SHORT "E" WORDS

Answer the riddles. Use one word from the short "e" list.
Write the word on the line.

tent

sled

hen

pen

cent

bell

belt

bed

nest

leg

desk

ten

1. You ride on me in winter. _____

2. Write with me. _____

3. Sleep in me outdoors. _____

4. I can ring. _____

5. Hop on me. _____

6. I come after nine. _____

7. I lay eggs. _____

8. Put papers on me. _____

9. I hold up your pants. _____

10. Dream on me. _____

11. Ten of me make a dime. _____

12. Baby birds grow in me. _____

My name is Fred. Does that mean that I'm a short "e" word?

SHORT "I" WORDS

Fill in the blanks with "i" to make silly sentences.
Read the sentences to a friend.

1. I h__d the l__d, I d__d.
2. I w__ll f__ll the p__ll with d__ll.
3. The w__tch fell in the d__tch with her sw__tch.
4. I w__sh the f__sh were st__ll in the d__sh.
5. Please l__ft the g__ft over the r__ft.
6. "You're a p__p," said the l__p to the h__p as
   they took a s__p.
7. The b__g p__g had on a w__g as he ate a f__g.
8. He l__t up the p__t to make __t f__t to s__t __n.

Add the beginning letter to make the same words that are
in the sentences above.

___id	___ill	___ish	___it
___id	___ill	___ish	___it
___id	___ill	___ish	___it
	___ill		___it

SHORT "O" WORDS

Add an "o" to these letters to make words.
Write the word in the blank space.

b__p _____   d__ck _____   c__t _____

c__p _____   l__ck _____   d__t _____

h__p _____   m__ck _____   g__t _____

m__p _____   r__ck _____   h__t _____

p__p _____   s__ck _____   l__t _____

t__p _____   t__ck _____   p__t _____

SILLY SENTENCES

Add an "o" to make short vowel words.

1. The c__p put the m__p on t__p of P__p!
2. I g__t a r__ck in my s__ck at the d__ck.
3. I have n__t g__t a h__t p__t on my c__t.

SHORT "U" WORDS

Read the short "u" words inside the umbrella.

Write two pairs that rhyme.

_____ _____

_____ _____

pup mud bug
fun gum mug
hug cup sun

Write the beginning letter for each picture to make a word.

1. ☐ + ☂ + ☐ _____

2. ☐ + ☂ + ☐ _____

3. ☐ + ☂ + ☐ _____

4. ☐ + ☂ + ☐ _____

5. ☐ + ☂ + ☐ _____

6. ☐ + ☂ + ☐ _____

7. ☐ + ☂ + ☐ _____

8. ☐ + ☂ + ☐ _____

9. ☐ + ☂ + ☐ _____

Running in the sun is fun!

SHORT VOWEL REVIEW

Add the right vowel to make a word.
Copy the words on the lines next to the correct vowel.

A _____

E _____

I _____

O _____

U _____

p__n
c__t

d__g   h__t

p__g
h__t

b__s

h__n
r__d

b__nd
b__ck

n__t

t__b

g__n

l__g

b__d

h__ll

s__ck

t__p
p__p

LONG "A" WORDS

When an "a" is followed by a "y" or an "i," it says its own name.

Using the words in the snail, help her get to the pail by writing the words on the line.

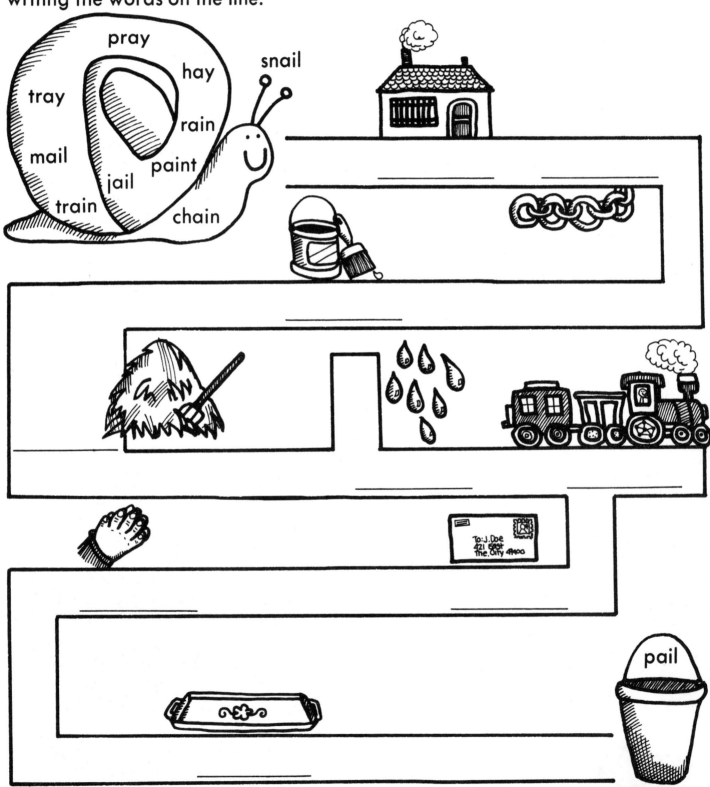

THE MAGIC "E"

Add "e" to the word and make a new word with a long vowel sound.

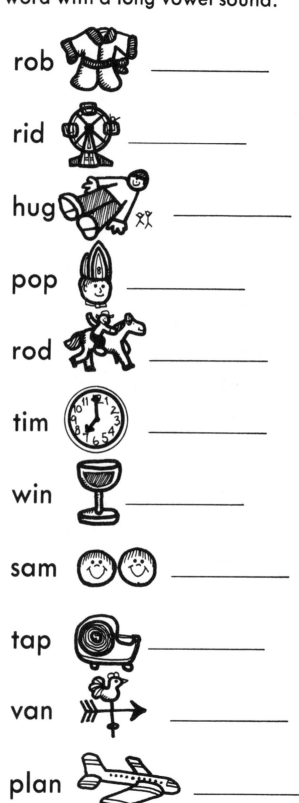

can   _____

cub   _____

cut   _____

pan   _____

tub   _____

dim   _____

cap   _____

pin   _____

not   _____

kit   _____

din   _____

slid   _____

rob   _____

rid   _____

hug   _____

pop   _____

rod   _____

tim   _____

win   _____

sam   _____

tap   _____

van   _____

plan   _____

plum   _____

LONG "E" WORDS

Long "e" sounds are made by "ea," "ee," or "ey." Color the long "e" words grey to make a picture.

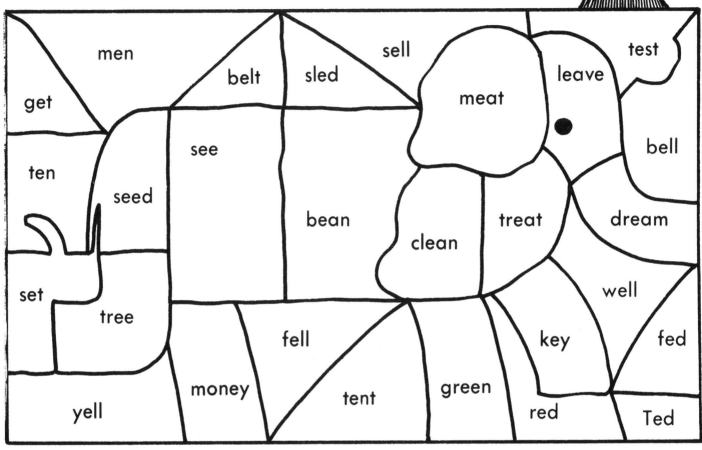

men

sell

test

belt   sled   leave

get   meat

see   bell

ten
                            treat   dream
seed   bean
                clean

set
tree   fell   well

        money   key   fed

yell   tent   green

                    red   Ted

Write the long "e" words on the lines below.

_____   _____

_____   _____

_____   _____

_____   _____

_____   _____

This is the greenest bean I've ever seen!

170

LONG "I" WORDS

The sound of "i" can be in a word as "ie" or "igh."
Sometimes a "y" sounds like "i."

Color the long "i" words in red and those that are not long "i" in blue.

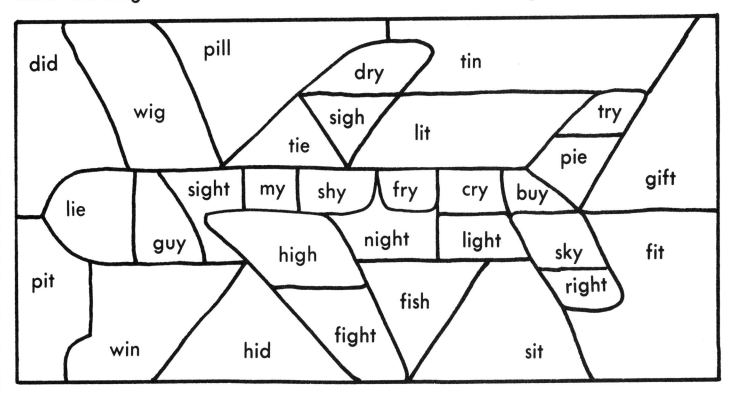

Write the long "i" words on the lines below.

uy	ie	igh

_____ _____ _____ _____

_____ _____ _____ _____

		y	

_____ _____

_____ _____ _____

LONG "O" WORDS

toast boat toad

road goat soap

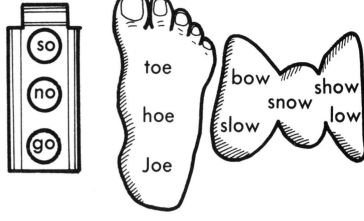

List the two letter words.

_____

_____

_____

List the three letter words.

_____   _____

_____   _____

_____

List all the "oa" words.

_____

_____

_____

_____

List all the "ow" words.

_____

_____

_____

No way can we go to the show when our money is so low, you know.

172

LONG "U" WORDS

In order to say its name, "u" likes an "e" on the end.

U-E

h__ge _____   r__de _____

c__be _____   t__ne _____

d__ne _____   c__te _____

t__be _____   f__me _____

U-I

It likes to be with "i" as in:

fr__ __t _____   j__ __ce _____   s__ __t _____

But "q" never goes without "u."   Try these words.

QU

q__eer _____   sq__ash _____

q__ick _____   sq__eal _____

q__ake _____   sq__eak _____

q__ilt _____   sq__ish _____

q__ack _____   sq__int _____

I don't mean to be rude, but I could really use a rest!

BE SMART
MAKE WORDS USING THESE ENDINGS

old

b _____
c _____
f _____
h _____
m _____
s _____
t _____

ank

b _____
d _____
l _____
r _____
s _____
fr _____
sp _____
bl _____
th _____
cr _____
dr _____

ink

l _____
m _____
r _____
s _____
w _____
p _____
th _____
bl _____

ick

D _____
h _____
l _____
p _____
s _____
t _____
w _____
cl _____
sl _____
br _____
tr _____
st _____

ing

k _____
r _____
s _____
w _____
cl _____
br _____
str _____
fl _____
spr _____
th _____

ang

b _____
f _____
h _____
r _____
s _____

ake

b _____
c _____
f _____
J _____
l _____
m _____
r _____
s _____
t _____
w _____
fl _____
br _____
st _____

ate

d _____
f _____
h _____
l _____
m _____
r _____
pl _____
cr _____
sk _____

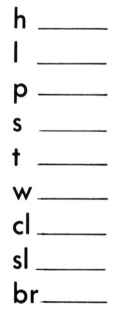

Look at all these new words you made!

174

THE "L" BLENDS

"L" likes to be next to these consonants.

Make words using these "l" blends. Fill in the blanks.
Then write the words on the line. Say the words.

bl

____ock   _____

____ess   _____

____ink   _____

____ow   _____

gl

____ad   _____

____ass   _____

____obe   _____

____itter   _____

cl

____own   _____

____ock   _____

____ub   _____

____ass   _____

pl

____an   _____

____ay   _____

____us   _____

____ant   _____

fl

____ower   _____

____ag   _____

____y   _____

____ash   _____

sl

____ip   _____

____eep   _____

____im   _____

____acks   _____

THE "S" BLENDS

Draw a line under two endings that make a word using the beginning letters. Say the words. The first one is done for you.

sk	ock	**spr**	ot	**scr**	ing
	ime		ay		am
	<u>ate</u>		ing		eam
	<u>in</u>		ub		ank

sp	eed	**sc**	alp	**squ**	ish
	ash		est		am
	ill		ale		eak
	one		art		ay

st	ing	**str**	ike	**spl**	it
	amp		ame		ing
	ike		og		ash
	ame		eet		ug

sl	eep	**sn**	ess	**sh**	ang
	ak		ap		eet
	aunt		ail		unk
	am		eat		ame

sm	oke	**sw**	ip	**shr**	one
	ick		oan		en
	ell		eet		ink
	one		im		ub

THE "R" BLENDS

Color the "r" blends green to make a picture.

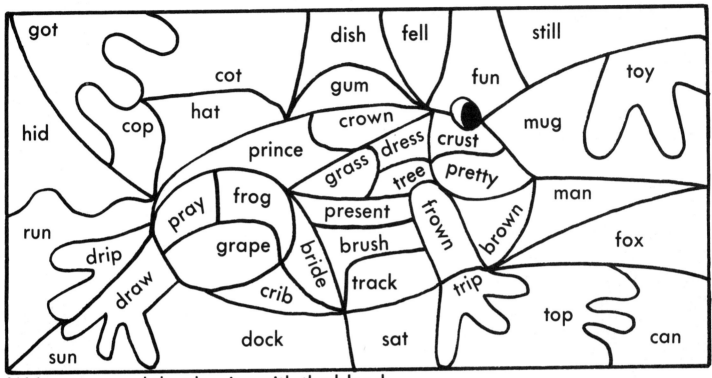

got · cot · dish · fell · still · toy · hat · cop · gum · fun · mug · hid · crown · crust · prince · grass · dress · pretty · man · pray · frog · tree · present · frown · brown · run · grape · brush · fox · drip · bride · track · trip · draw · crib · dock · sat · top · can · sun

Write one word that begins with the blend.

br _____

fr _____

pr _____

cr _____

gr _____

tr _____

dr _____

I prefer a sandwich made on brown bread for lunch.

I'm trying fruit for lunch this week.

BLENDS REVIEW

Make a new word by adding the ending to the blend. Say the words. The first one is done for you.

gray	**pr**ay	**tr**_____	**pl**_____
cry	**fr**_____	**fl**_____	**sk**_____
crash	**tr**_____	**cl**_____	**sm**_____
drip	**fl**_____	**sl**_____	**sk**_____
grow	**bl**_____	**cr**_____	**sl**_____
block	**cr**_____	**cl**_____	**sm**_____
brown	**dr**_____	**fr**_____	**cl**_____
skill	**sp**_____	**st**_____	**gr**_____
brush	**bl**_____	**cr**_____	**pl**_____
crack	**tr**_____	**bl**_____	**st**_____
bring	**cl**_____	**fl**_____	**st**_____
frog	**sm**_____	**cl**_____	**fl**_____

That wasn't bad at all, was it?

SH CH TH WH

Some letters make a new sound when they're put together. Do these letters go at the beginning or at the end ?

Write the word on the line.

__sh__	__ch__	__th__	__wh__
ake _shake_	in _chin_	ink _think_	eat _wheat_
wa _____	por _____	ird _____	eel _____
op _____	ild _____	mou_____	ale _____
ed _____	ea _____	umb_____	ip _____
fi _____	ri _____	ba _____	istle_____
ade_____	in _____	clo _____	y _____
ell _____	su _____	bo _____	ich _____
irt _____	whi_____	wor_____	at _____
fre _____	erry_____	sou_____	ile _____
ca _____	wat _____	pa _____	ite _____
eep_____	air _____	ick _____	isker_____
ip _____	eese_____	nor _____	ere _____

179

HELP THE BOY

The sound of "oi" in oil and "oy" in boy is the same.

Write an "oi" or an "oy" in each word to go through the path to the toy plane.

b__ __

p__ __nt

br__ __l

v__ __d

sp__ __l

c__ __

s__ __l

n__ __se

m__ __st

h__ __st

__ __l

ch__ __ce

j__ __n

j__ __

c__ __n

b__ __l

v__ __ce

t__ __

RIDDLES

Some words have the same vowel sound, but it's made with different letters.

moon

suit

glue

blew

Answer the riddles using words from the list. Write the word on the line.

moose
blue
pew
dew
broom
tooth
true
chew
pool
stool
glue
school

1. The color of the sky. _____

2. You find me on the grass in the morning. _____

3. Stick things together with me. _____

4. A big animal with antlers. _____

5. The name of a seat in church. _____

6. What you do with gum. _____

7. You can sit on me. _____

8. Sweep the floor with me. _____

9. The opposite of false. _____

10. Brush me twice a day. _____

11. This is where you learn every day. _____

12. You can swim in me. _____

SILLY SENTENCES

The sound of "ou" as in mouse and "ow" as in owl are the same.

Fill in the blanks with "ou" or "ow."

1. A Boy Sc __ __ t will not p __ __ t or fr __ __ n.

2. The br __ __ n tr __ __ t cannot dr __ __ n in water.

3. The h __ __ nd said " __ __ ch" with a l __ __ d h __ __ l!

4. The cl __ __ n sat d __ __ n ar __ __ nd the fl __ __ ers.

5. C __ __ nt the cr __ __ d d __ __ n at the r __ __ nd t __ __ er.

6. The cr __ __ n is h __ __ the king ann __ __ nces his p __ __ er.

7. My m __ __ th has a s __ __ r taste.

8. I f __ __ nd a m __ __ se in my h __ __ se under the c __ __ ch.

Write 4 "ou" words.

_____

_____

_____

_____

Write 4 "ow" words.

_____

_____

_____

_____

182

SILENT LETTERS

Sometimes the letters l, k, w, h, t, b, and gh are silent.
Add the silent letters, then write the word on the line.

(w)

__ rap _____

__ rong _____

__ rite _____

(gh)

hi __ __ _____

nau __ __ ty _____

ni __ __ t _____

(b)

dum __ _____

thum __ _____

crum __ _____

(t)

ca __ ch _____

ma __ ch _____

wi __ ch _____

(k)

__ nob _____

__ nit _____

__ nee _____

shhhhhh!

(l)

wa __ k _____

sta __ k _____

ta __ k _____

(h)

__ onest _____

__ our _____

g __ ost _____

See if you can still find the word when they're mixed up.

cha __ k _____

__ nock _____

__ now _____

fi __ __ t _____

com __ _____

ca __ f _____

__ new _____

lam __ _____

__ rite _____

ki __ chen _____

scra __ ch _____

ri __ __ t _____

"R" MAKES IT DIFFERENT

Whenever an "r" comes next to a vowel, it makes the sound different. Put either <u>ar</u>, <u>er</u>, <u>ir</u>, <u>or</u>, or <u>ur</u> in the blanks to make a story. Check your answers to make sure they're correct.

A g__ __l with a c__ __l on h__ __ f__ __ehead was going to the p__ __k. She took h__ __ p__ __se and w__ __e sh__ __ts and a sh__ __t. When she left her front p__ __ch, a man in a d__ __k c__ __ blew his h__ __n. It was h__ __ fath__ __. He thought his daught__ __ was v__ __y sm__ __t and ch__ __ming.

At the p__ __k there was a b__ __n with f__ __m animals in it. Fath__ __ let h__ __ ride a h__ __se. She fell off and was h__ __t. A n__ __se fixed her __ __m. Fath__ __ and daught__ __ then went to the p__ __k st__ __e and bought some popc__ __n.
She was th__ __sty so she had an __ __ange drink.

When they got home, Moth__ __ had a b__ __thday p__ __ty f__ __ h__ __. It was a wond__ __ful b__ __thday!

184

C AND G

I sound like "k" before these letters.

A O U

I sound like "s" before these letters.

I E Y

Copy the words. Say them as you write.

cat _____

cot _____

candy _____

coffee _____

could _____

cup _____

city _____

cigar _____

lace _____

face _____

ice _____

cycle _____

Then there's circus _____.

I sound like the "g" in goat before these letters.

A O U

I usually sound like "j" before these letters.

I E Y

Copy the words. Say them as you write.

gas _____

gum _____

go _____

good _____

get _____

gun _____

gym _____

gem _____

magic _____

gentle _____

large _____

page _____

Then there's garbage _____.

USE AN APOSTROPHE TO MAKE WORDS SMALLER

Match the two words with the short one.   Write the contraction on the line.
The first one is done for you.

are not	I'll	aren't
you will	can't	_____
they are	aren't	_____
I have	they're	_____
can not	you'll	_____
he is	I've	_____
could not	we've	_____
I will	he's	_____
we have	couldn't	_____
is not	we're	_____
did not	they'll	_____
they will	isn't	_____
we are	didn't	_____

How did you do on this page?

MAKE ONE WORD OUT OF TWO

Look at the pictures. Then write the compound word on the line.

	_____
	_____
	_____
	_____
	_____
	_____
	_____
	_____
	_____
	_____
	_____
	_____
	_____

HOW DO YOU HANDLE MORE THAN ONE?

Sometimes you add "s." Write the word, adding "<u>s</u>."

book _____   clock _____   mother _____

hand _____   flower _____   doll _____

When the word ends in "x," "ss," "ch," or "sh," you add "<u>es</u>."

box _____   witch _____   dish _____

dress _____   wish _____   church _____

When the word ends in "y," usually you change the "y" to "i" and add "<u>es</u>."

baby _____   pony _____   fairy _____

penny _____   berry _____   city _____

When the word ends in "f," you change the "f" to "v" and add "<u>es</u>."

leaf _____   wife _____   knife _____

Our teacher knows how to handle more than one!

ENDINGS ARE DIFFERENT

Do what it tells you.

Use a double consonant before adding "ing" when a verb ends in a consonant preceded by a single vowel.

Just add "ing."

think _____

sing _____

work _____

yell _____

Drop "e" and add "ing."

love _____

save _____

make _____

come _____

run _____

swim _____

jog _____

step _____

Sometimes you just add a suffix.

Add "ful."

wonder _____

care _____

cup _____

thank _____

help _____

pain _____

Add "er" or "est."

small _____

fast _____

slow _____

old _____

hard _____

kind _____

Add "ness" or "less."

sick _____

good _____

care _____

hard _____

kind _____

help _____

Hmmmm... endings ARE different!

BEGINNINGS
MAKE A DIFFERENCE

Do the word puzzle.

"Un" in front of a word means "not."

u	n					
u	n					
u	n					
u	n					
u	n					
u	n					

1. not happy

2. not able

3. not safe

4. not kind

5. not even

6. not tied

"Mis" in front of a word means "wrong."

m	i	s					
m	i	s					
m	i	s					
m	i	s					
m	i	s					
m	i	s					

1. wrong fit

2. wrong place

3. wrong deal

4. wrong fire

5. wrong count

6. wrong spell

Page 161

bear
cat
dog
fish
goat
horse
jaguar
kangaroo
lion
mouse
nightingale
pig
quail
rabbit
seal
tiger
vulture
walrus
fox
yak
zebra

Page 162

1. at, as, an, am
2. fan, had, ant, cat

bat	ham	ran	bad
hat	Sam	man	dad
mat	ram	tan	had
pat	jam	pan	mad
sat	dam	fan	lad

Page 163

1. sled
2. pen
3. tent
4. bell
5. leg
6. ten
7. hen
8. desk
9. belt
10. bed
11. cent
12. nest

Page 164

1. I hid the lid, I did.
2. I will fill the pill with dill.
3. The witch fell in the ditch with her switch.
4. I wish the fish were still in the dish.
5. Please lift the gift over the rift.
6. "You're a pip," said the lip to the hip as they took a sip.
7. The big pig had on a wig as he ate a fig.
8. He lit up the pit to make it fit to sit in.

hid	will	wish	lit
lid	fill	fish	pit
did	pill	dish	fit
	dill		sit

Page 165

1. The cop put the mop on top of Pop!
2. I got a rock in my sock at the dock.
3. I have not got a hot pot on my cot.

Page 166

pup, cup
bug, mug, hug
fun, sun
1. pup
2. gum
3. mug
4. fun
5. hug
6. bug
7. cup
8. sun
9. mud

Page 167

A	I	U
pan	pig	bus
cat	hit	gun
band	hill	nut
back	sick	tub
E	O	
hen	dog	
red	hot	
bed	top	
leg	pop	

Page 168

jail
chain
paint
hay
rain
train
mail
pray
tray

Page 169

Automatic
fill-in.

Page 170

meat
clean
leave
green
money
bean
seed
see
key
treat
tree
dream

Page 171

uy	y
guy	my
buy	shy
igh	try
high	fry
night	sky
light	dry
fight	cry
sight	ie
sigh	lie
right	pie
	tie

Page 172

Two letter
so
no
go
Three letter
toe
hoe
Joe
low
bow

ow	oa
slow	toast
bow	road
snow	boat
show	goat
low	toad
	soap

Page 173

Automatic fill-in.

Page 174

Automatic fill-in.

Page 175

Automatic fill-in.

Page 176

skate
skin
speed
spill
sting
stamp
sleep
slam
smoke
smell

spray
spring
scalp
scale
strike
street
snap
snail
sweet
swim

scram
scream
squish
squeak
split
splash
sheet
shame
shrink
shrub

Page 177

br	cr
brown	crib
bride	crust
brush	crown
dr	**fr**
drip	frown
draw	frog
dress	**pr**
gr	pretty
grape	pray
grass	prince
tr	present
trip	
tree	
track	

Page 178

Automatic fill-in.

Page 179

sh	ch	th	wh
wash	porch	third	wheel
shop	child	mouth	whale
shed	each	thumb	whip
fish	rich	bath	whistle
shade	chin or inch	cloth	why
shell	such	both	which
shirt	which	worth	what
fresh	cherry	south	while
cash	watch	path	white
sheep	chair	thick	whisker
ship	cheese	north	where

Page 180

boy	hoist
point	oil
broil	choice
noise	coin
soil	joy
coy	join
spoil	boil
void	voice
moist	toy

Page 181

1. blue
2. dew
3. glue
4. moose
5. pew
6. chew
7. stool
8. broom
9. true
10. tooth
11. school
12. pool

Page 182

1. A Boy Scout will not pout or frown.
2. The brown trout cannot drown in water.
3. The hound said "Ouch" with a loud howl!
4. The clown sat down around the flowers.
5. Count the crowd down at the round tower.
6. The crown is how the king announces his power.
7. My mouth has a sour taste.
8. I found a mouse in my house under the couch.

Scout	house	frown	crown
pout	couch	brown	how
trout	around	drown	power
hound	count	howl	down
loud	sour	clown	
ouch	mouth	flowers	
announces	mouse	crowd	
found		tower	

Page 183

Automatic fill-in.
chalk
knock
know
fight
comb
calf
knew
lamb
write
kitchen
scratch
right

Page 184

A girl with a curl on her forehead was going to the park. She took her purse and wore shorts and a shirt. When she left her front porch, a man in a dark car blew his horn. It was her father. He thought his daughter was very smart and charming.

At the park there was a barn with farm animals in it. Father let her ride a horse. She fell off and was hurt. A nurse fixed her arm. Father and daughter then went to the park store and bought some popcorn. She was thirsty, so she had an orange drink.

When they got home, Mother had a birthday party for her. It was a wonderful birthday!

Page 185

Automatic fill-in.

Page 186

are not – aren't
you will – you'll
they are – they're
I have – I've
can not – can't
he is – he's
could not – couldn't
I will – I'll
we have – we've
is not – isn't
did not – didn't
they will – they'll
we are – we're

Page 187

football
lighthouse
rainbow
fireman
doorbell
pancake
starfish
cowboy
birdhouse
watchdog
stepladder
eardrum
toothbrush

Page 188

Automatic fill-in.

Page 189

Automatic fill-in.

Page 190

unhappy
unable
unsafe
unkind
uneven
untied
misfit
misplace
misdeal
misfire
miscount
misspell

Draw a line from each word to its picture.

throw

catch

point

pick

feel

Write a correct word on each line.
Use the words from above.

1. I can _____ the football.

2. Will Sheila _____ the baseball?

3. My brother will _____ apples today.

4. Does a rabbit _____ soft and fluffy?

5. Did he _____ his finger at me?

Draw a line from each word to its picture.

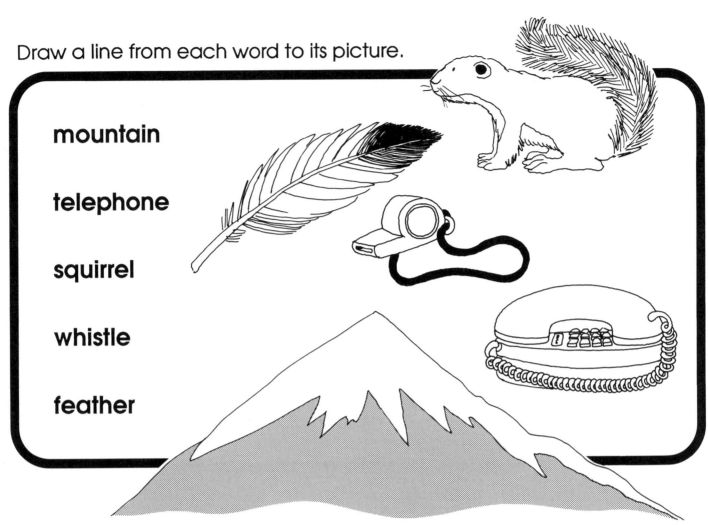

mountain

telephone

squirrel

whistle

feather

Write the correct word on each line.
Use the words from above.

1. Ouch! That _____ tried to bite me!

2. An eagle's _____ floated to the ground.

3. Jill climbed a _____ today.

4. We all heard the _____ ring.

5. The coach blew the _____ three times.

Some words mean almost the same thing.
Little means the same as **small**.
Circle the word that means the **same as** the first word.

1. **afraid**   silly   scared   reach

2. **mad**   angry   wave   splash

3. **yell**   sea   shout   quiet

4. **wise**   wait   magic   smart

5. **keep**   save   bow   move

6. **unhappy**   noise   thumb   sad

Circle the correct word to end the sentence.

1. **Sudden** is the same as   smile   poor   quick

2. A **tiny** toy is very   small   round   old

3. A **plate** is a   spoon   shoe   dish

4. The **woods** are the   forest   fields   barn

5. To **view** something is to   help   cry   see

6. If you are filled with **joy**, you are   purple   happy   silly

Circle the word that means the **same as** the first word.

1. **also**   giant   inside   too

2. **wash**   clean   chase   dot

3. **near**   idea   close   loud

4. **merry**   story   live   happy

5. **throw**   please   toss   hop

6. **picture**   photo   point   camera

Circle the correct word to end the sentence.

1. **Beautiful** means   cold   lovely   more

2. A **pond** is a little   forest   lake   store

3. To **wish** is to   hope   jump   peek

4. To **end** is to   start   finish   yell

5. A **brook** is a   lake   flower   stream

6. A **part** of something is a   wall   pail   piece

Circle the word that means the **same as** the first word.

1. **bucket**   dish   pail   sponge

2. **pick**   choose   calf   care

3. **strange**   knock   most   queer

4. **quick**   wear   fast   late

5. **forest**   water   tree   woods

6. **stone**   stick   rock   mud

Circle the correct word to end the sentence.

1. To **place** is to   give   win   put

2. If you **shout**, you   yell   hide   throw

3. To **toss** is to   part   throw   find

4. When you **act**, you   smell   sit   pretend

5. To **go** is to   leave   cry   wait

6. To **keep** is to   burn   save   climb

Put together a word from each box to make one new word.
Write the new word on the line.

| ant | head |
| book | foot |

| phones | ball |
| eater | case |

headphones

_____

_____

_____

Take each word apart to make two words.

goldfish	=	_gold_	+	_fish_
butterfly	=	_____	+	_____
railroad	=	_____	+	_____
yourself	=	_____	+	_____
highway	=	_____	+	_____
wristwatch	=	_____	+	_____

Put together a word from each box to make one new word.
Write the new word on the line.

snow   sun

water   grape

_____

_____

glasses   fruit

melon   shoes

_____

_____

Take each word apart to make two words.

bedroom   =   _____ + _____

afternoon   =   _____ + _____

workbook   =   _____ + _____

fireplace   =   _____ + _____

anywhere   =   _____ + _____

shortstop   =   _____ + _____

Put together a word from each box to make one new word.
Write the new word on the line.

horse   bird

snap   box

shot   house

car   shoe

_____

_____

_____

_____

Take each word apart to make two words.

fingernail   =   _____ + _____

spaceship   =   _____ + _____

nearby   =   _____ + _____

sometimes   =   _____ + _____

superwoman   =   _____ + _____

blueberries =   _____ + _____

Some words mean opposite things.
Bad means the opposite of **good**.
Circle the word that means the **opposite** of the first word.

1. **dirty**	still	clean	wash
2. **same**	caught	some	different
3. **quick**	slow	drop	hurry
4. **noisy**	listen	busy	quiet
5. **sell**	need	buy	like
6. **remember**	forget	think	enough

Draw a line from each word to its **opposite.**

1. **good**	**narrow**
2. **high**	**weak**
3. **win**	**bad**
4. **wide**	**shout**
5. **whisper**	**low**
6. **strong**	**lose**

Circle the word that means the **opposite** of the first word.

1. **early**   late   last   excited

2. **hard**   line   twice   easy

3. **finish**   choose   begin   follow

4. **empty**   heavy   light   full

5. **many**   few   all   large

6. **everything**   elevator   nothing   sometime

Draw a line from each word to its **opposite**.

1. **wonderful**   **poor**

2. **straight**   **crooked**

3. **rich**   **pull**

4. **push**   **none**

5. **open**   **awful**

6. **every**   **close**

Circle the word that means the **opposite** of the first word.

1. **whisper**   say   cry   shout

2. **lose**   win   tight   count

3. **summer**   beach   winter   spring

4. **without**   happen   return   with

5. **awake**   asleep   tired   shall

6. **right**   high   low   wrong

Draw a line from each word to its **opposite**.

1. **loose**   **finish**

2. **correct**   **worst**

3. **save**   **tight**

4. **best**   **spend**

5. **begin**   **same**

6. **different**   **wrong**

Draw a line from each meaning to the correct word.

1. not the same; not alike   **quack**

2. greatest in number or size   **part**

3. the sound made by a duck   **different**

4. in what way   **how**

5. a piece of the whole   **read**

6. to understand written words   **most**

Unscramble the letters and write the correct word.

1. You walk up it.   **l i l h**   h i l l

2. frozen water   **c e i**   ___ ___ ___

3. It grows in the woods.   **r e t e**   ___ ___ ___ ___

4. You ride it to school.   **s u b**   ___ ___ ___

5. the doorway through a fence   **t e a g**   ___ ___ ___ ___

6. yellow food that grows on a cob   **r o c n**   ___ ___ ___ ___

Draw a line from each meaning to the correct word.

1. what is said in reply to a question   **flat**

2. letters sent through the post office   **honey**

3. the part of a building that is below the ground   **mail**

4. having a smooth and even top   **basement**

5. a covering for the hand   **answer**

6. sweet, thick syrup made by bees   **glove**

Unscramble the letters and write the correct word.

1. You hear with this.   **a r e**   ___ ___ ___

2. You lift with it.   **m a r**   ___ ___ ___

3. an animal that roars   **n o l i**   ___ ___ ___ ___

4. You do this to numbers.   **d a d**   ___ ___ ___

5. at this very minute   **w n o**   ___ ___ ___

6. Yum! Tastes good!   **e p i**   ___ ___ ___

Draw a line from each meaning to the correct word.

1. to move back and forth quickly   **wheel**

2. very active; stirred up   **bump**

3. to hit or knock against something   **excited**

4. very good; excellent   **library**

5. a place where books are kept   **wonderful**

6. a round thing that turns around its center   **shake**

Unscramble the letters and write the correct word.

1. It's in the sky.   **u n s**   ___ ___ ___

2. You eat from this.   **s h d i**   ___ ___ ___ ___

3. at the end of your leg   **t o f o**   ___ ___ ___ ___

4. You blow it.   **r o h n**   ___ ___ ___ ___

5. a number   **n e t**   ___ ___ ___

6. a clever red animal   **x f o**   ___ ___ ___

Circle the six words that tell something about **winter**.

ice
hot
mittens
animal

sled
book

airplane
skate

prize
other

snow
cold

Circle the six words that tell something about **indoors**.

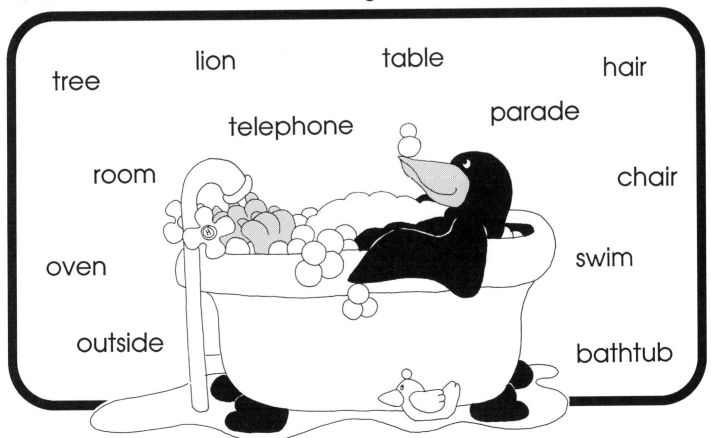

lion
table
hair

tree

telephone
parade

room
chair

oven
swim

outside
bathtub

Circle the six words that tell something about **feelings**.

uncle
sad
afraid
angry
splash
tent
proud
sorry
glad
piece
wheel
rocket

Circle the six words that tell something about **tools**.

robin
rake
hammer
rain
silk
screwdriver
apple
pond
broom
maybe
saw
shovel

208

Read each meaning.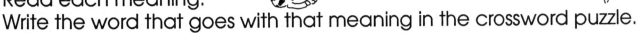
Write the word that goes with that meaning in the crossword puzzle.

DOWN

1. The land ___ground___

2. A short letter ___

3. Into ___

ACROSS

2. A person who lives nearby ___

4. To come up after being thrown down ___

5. A thing made for climbing ___

bounce

inside

note

ground

neighbor

ladder

Read each meaning.
Write the word that goes with that meaning in the crossword puzzle.

DOWN

1. Not curving _____

2. Boys, girls, women, and men _____

ACROSS

3. A person who teaches _____

4. To move smoothly _____

5. Way up above the ground _____

6. The hard parts of the mouth, used for chewing _____

high

teeth

people

slide

straight

teacher

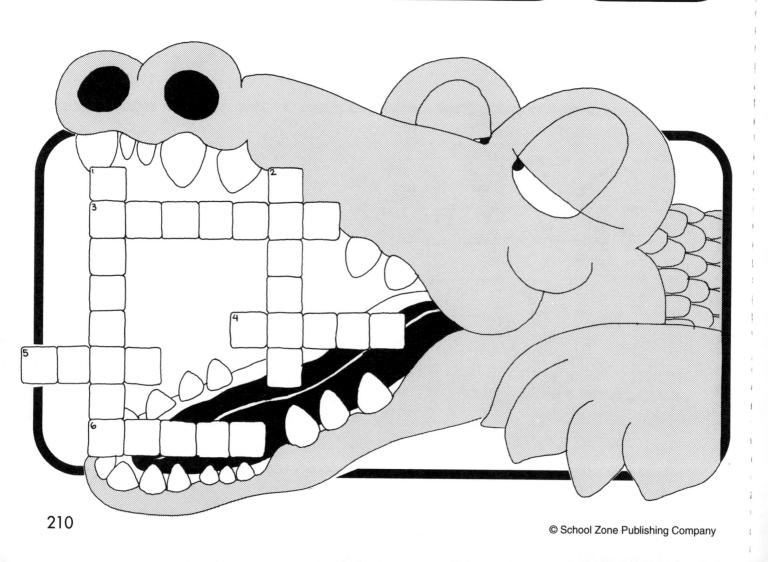

Some words sound alike.
Sun sounds like **son**. **Hour** sounds like **our**.
Circle the word that **sounds like** the first word.

1. **dear**	dare	does	deer
2. **knows**	nose	knew	knees
3. **pair**	poor	pear	part
4. **sea**	seal	seem	see
5. **tail**	tale	tall	tell
6. **threw**	true	through	throw

Read each sentence.
Only one of the bold words is correct.
Circle the correct word.

1. The **dear deer** ran through the woods.

2. The lion bit the tiger's **tail tale**.

3. Mickey broke his **knows nose** skating.

4. Whales live in the **sea see**.

5. The train zoomed **through threw** the tunnel.

6. Zora lost seven **pears pairs** of gloves.

Circle the word that **sounds like** the first word.

1. **whole** whale wall hole

2. **high** low hi night

3. **aunt** and hunt ant

4. **close** clothes cloth class

5. **night** not knot knight

6. **eight** eat ate even

Read each sentence.
Only one of the bold words is correct.
Circle the correct word.

1. Steven counted **eight ate** candles.

2. Hurry! **Clothes Close** the door!

3. My **aunt ant** baked this cake.

4. The raccoon ate the **whole hole** pie.

5. We are leaving for vacation tomorrow **knight night**.

6. How **hi high** is the diving board?

212

Some words have more than one meaning.
A **park** is a place to walk and play. To **park** a car is to move it into a spot.
Write the letter of each meaning next to the correct sentence.

A. **left**   a direction; the opposite of right
B. **left**   went away from
C. **iron**   a hard gray metal found in rocks
D. **iron**   to press; to make smooth
E. **mean**   not kind; cruel
F. **mean**   to have as a purpose; to have as a meaning

_____E_____ Steve was **mean** to me today.
_____ We **left** the dogs at home.
_____ This mountain is full of **iron**.
_____ The giant turned **left**.
_____ What does "poncho" **mean**?
_____ Can Dad **iron** a shirt?

Can you answer each riddle?
Write the answer on the line.

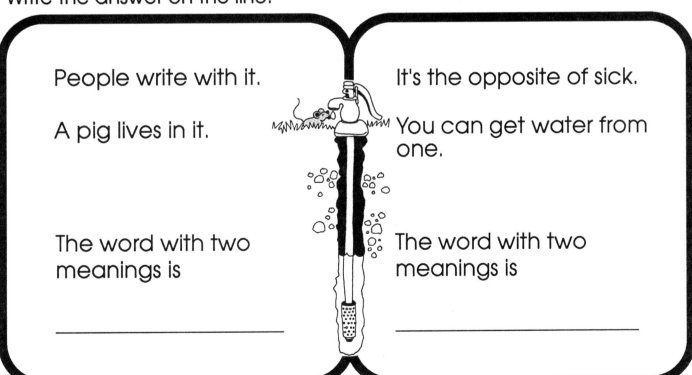

People write with it.

A pig lives in it.

The word with two meanings is

_____

It's the opposite of sick.

You can get water from one.

The word with two meanings is

_____

Some words have more than one meaning.
A **park** is a place to walk and play. To **park** a car is to move it into a spot.
Write the letter of each meaning next to the correct sentence.

A. **duck**   a water bird with webbed feet
B. **duck**   to lower the head or the body quickly
C. **can**   to be able to
D. **can**   a thing which holds food; made of metal
E. **play**   to take part in a game; to do something for fun
F. **play**   a story acted on a stage

_____   "**Duck!**" shouted the clown as he threw a dish.
_____   I dropped the **can** on my toe.
_____   Young animals like to **play**.
_____   **Can** bears climb trees?
_____   My sister is the star of the **play**.
_____   The **duck** laid six eggs.

Can you answer each riddle?
Write the answer on the line.

A train runs down it.

Your footprint leaves one in the snow.

The word with two meanings is

_____

It's at the end of your leg.

Twelve inches are one.

The word with two meanings is

_____

Some words have more than one meaning.
A **park** is a place to walk and play. To **park** a car is to move it into a spot.
Write the letter of each meaning next to the correct sentence.

A. **rest**   to stop doing something and relax
B. **rest**   the part that is left over
C. **ring**   to make a sound like a bell
D. **ring**   jewelry worn on a finger
E. **watch**   a thing that tells time
F. **watch**   a time during which a person guards something

_____   "Let Marbles **rest**," warned Dad.
_____   The sailor fell asleep during his **watch**.
_____   Mom's **ring** rolled down the drain.
_____   Listen! I heard the telephone **ring**.
_____   Felicia took two kittens and I took the **rest**.
_____   We bought Chung a **watch** for his birthday.

Can you answer each riddle?
Write the answer on the line.

It's the sound a balloon makes when it breaks.

Or, you might drink it.

The word with two meanings is

_____

This is a size.

This might also come down the beanstalk after Jack.

The word with two meanings is

_____

Some words have more than one meaning.
A **park** is a place to walk and play. To **park** a car is to move it into a spot.
Write the letter of each meaning next to the correct sentence.

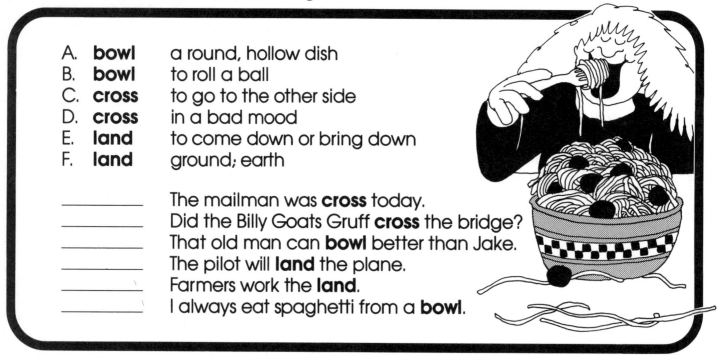

A. **bowl**   a round, hollow dish
B. **bowl**   to roll a ball
C. **cross**   to go to the other side
D. **cross**   in a bad mood
E. **land**   to come down or bring down
F. **land**   ground; earth

_____   The mailman was **cross** today.
_____   Did the Billy Goats Gruff **cross** the bridge?
_____   That old man can **bowl** better than Jake.
_____   The pilot will **land** the plane.
_____   Farmers work the **land**.
_____   I always eat spaghetti from a **bowl**.

Can you answer each riddle?
Write the answer on the line.

I am part of the alphabet!

I am something you get in the mail.

The word with two meanings is

_____

You can carry things in it.

A basketball player gets points for it.

The word with two meanings is

_____

216

Read each dictionary meaning below.
Write the correct word under each picture.

dormouse   a small animal something like a squirrel

gear   a wheel with parts that stick out

gopher   a small animal something like a chipmunk; it has large pouches in its cheeks

harp   a large musical instrument with strings; it stands upright

hogan   a house made of stones or logs with a roof of dirt

outrigger   a float that keeps a canoe from tipping over

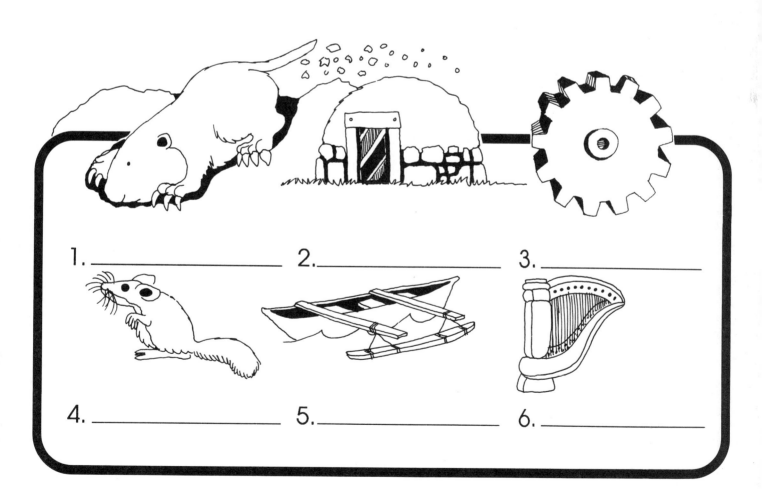

1. _____   2. _____   3. _____

4. _____   5. _____   6. _____

Read each dictionary meaning below.
Write the correct word under each picture.

quiver   a case for holding arrows

lynx   a large, wild cat with a short tail

manger   a large box from which cows are fed

milestone   a stone marker that tells how far away a place is

poncho   a covering with a hole in the middle and no sleeves

fisher   an animal with a long thin body and thick fur

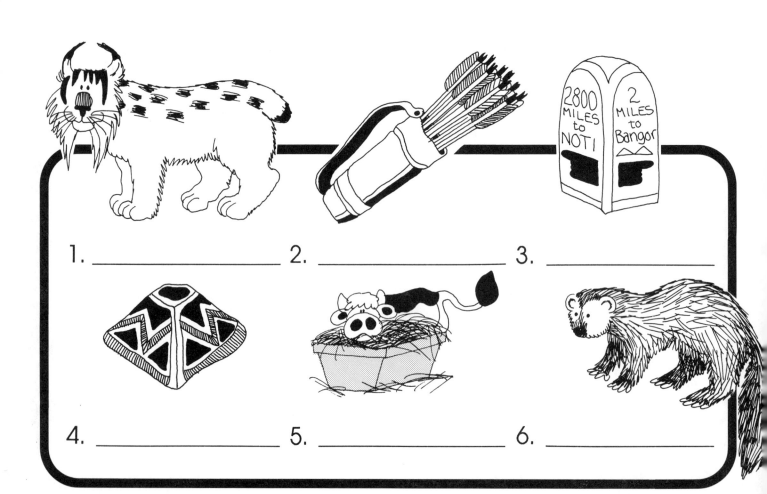

1. _____   2. _____   3. _____

4. _____   5. _____   6. _____

Read the story.

Hobart the Rotten Robot

    Cindy heard a loud **noise**. She looked over her shoulder at the door. The door was still shut and **locked**. But she could hear somebody **pounding** on the door.

    "Beep! Let me in, Cindy. Beep."

    It was Hobart the Robot. Cindy would not let him in. If Cindy let Hobart in, Hobart would take the controls away from her. Hobart would turn the **spaceship** around and fly back to the **planet** Rotten. You see, Hobart was a Rotten **robot**, and Rotten robots always tried to take over spaceships.

    "Beep! Let me in, Cindy. Beep."

    "Never," shouted Cindy. "I'm taking the spaceship back to Earth."

Read the story again.
Then write each bold word on the correct line.

1. _____ kept closed with a fastener

2. _____ a "ship" for flying beyond Earth

3. _____ hitting hard against something

4. _____ a heavenly body such as Earth

5. _____ a machine that can do work

6. _____ a sound, often loud or unpleasant

Read the story.

Make Me a Blanket

Do you read the comics? Maybe you read *Peanuts*. In *Peanuts*, Linus almost always carries a **blanket**. His blanket might be made of wool. Blankets can be made from many different things. Wool, for example, comes from a sheep's hair. A wool blanket is very **warm**.

Some blankets are made from cotton. Cotton comes from a plant. Long **ago**, some blankets were made from **leather**. Leather is what shoes are made of today. It comes from animal skins.

The first blankets were made from grass or **leaves**. People just lay down on the ground and covered themselves with leaves and went to **sleep**. Do you think Linus would like a blanket made from leaves?

Read the story again.
Then write each bold word on the correct line.

1. _____ resting while not awake

2. _____ a covering for a bed

3. _____ a little bit hot, but not very hot

4. _____ before this time

5. _____ usually brown, it comes from animal skins

6. _____ the parts of a plant that grow from the stem

220

Read the story.

A Berry Good Mistake

Bear loved strawberries and blueberries. She loved raspberries and blackberries. Bear was going to **pick** berries. "I want a **heap** of berries," she said. "I want to eat them all at once!"

So all day long Bear picked berries. She put them in a big basket. "When I get home, I'll eat all my berries at once. Yum!"

But when Bear got home, she was too tired to eat. "I'll hide my berries," she said. So she put them on a piece of **dough**. She covered them with another piece of dough. Then she put the berries in the **oven** to hide them even more.

Bear fell asleep. When she woke up, she smelled something. Sniff! Sniff! She ran to the oven. It was her berries! What had happened? The dough was all cooked. The **berries** were inside the dough. What had happened to her wonderful pile of berries?

Bear bit into the dough. She tasted the berries. "Oh, yum!" she said. "Oh, yummy, yum! I don't know what I did, but I think I'll call it **pie**."

Read the story again.
Then write each bold word on the correct line.

1. _____   a place where things are baked

2. _____   choose

3. _____   flour and water mixed together

4. _____   a big pile

5. _____   very small juicy fruits

6. _____   cooked crusts filled with fruit or other things

Read the story.

Three, Four, Five, Six Sides

Shapes are very interesting. Many shapes have names. The names usually come from the number of sides a shape has. You probably know that a shape with three sides is called a **triangle**. A shape with four sides is called a **rectangle**.

A **square** is a special kind of rectangle – all four of its sides are the same length. Another special rectangle is the **diamond**. The diamond has four equal sides, but the four sides do not make a box shape the way a square does.

Those are the easy shapes that most people know. But what is a shape with five sides called? It's called a **pentagon**. And a shape with six sides is called a **hexagon**.

Read the story again.
Then write each bold word on the correct line.

1. _____ ■   4. _____ ▮

2. _____ ⬟   5. _____ ⬡

3. _____ ▲   6. _____ ◆

Page 193
Bottom
1. catch – throw
2. throw – catch
3. pick – throw – catch
4. feel
5. point

Page 194
Bottom
1. squirrel
2. feather
3. mountain
4. telephone
5. whistle

Page 195
Top
1. scared
2. angry
3. shout
4. smart
5. save
6. sad

Bottom
1. quick
2. small
3. dish
4. forest
5. see
6. happy

Page 196
Top
1. too
2. clean
3. close
4. happy
5. toss
6. photo

Bottom
1. lovely
2. lake
3. hope
4. finish
5. stream
6. piece

Page 197
Top
1. pail
2. choose
3. queer
4. fast
5. woods
6. rock

Bottom
1. put
2. yell
3. throw
4. pretend
5. leave
6. save

Page 198
Top
headphones
bookcase
anteater
football

Bottom
gold + fish
butter + fly
rail + road
your + self
high + way
wrist + watch

Page 199
Top
snowshoes
watermelon
sunglasses
grapefruit

Bottom
bed + room
after + noon
work + book
fire + place
any + where
short + stop

Page 200
Top
horseshoe
birdhouse
snapshot
boxcar

Bottom
finger + nail
space + ship
near + by
some + times
super + woman
blue + berries

Page 201
Top
1. clean
2. different
3. slow
4. quiet
5. buy
6. forget

Bottom
1. bad
2. low
3. lose
4. narrow
5. shout
6. weak

Page 202
Top
1. late
2. easy
3. begin
4. full
5. few
6. nothing

Bottom
1. awful
2. crooked
3. poor
4. pull
5. close
6. none

Page 203
Top
1. shout
2. win
3. winter
4. with
5. asleep
6. wrong

Bottom
1. tight
2. wrong
3. spend
4. worst
5. finish
6. same

Page 204
Top
1. different
2. most
3. quack
4. how
5. part
6. read

Bottom
1. hill
2. ice
3. tree
4. bus
5. gate
6. corn

Page 205
Top
1. answer
2. mail
3. basement
4. flat
5. glove
6. honey

Bottom
1. ear
2. arm
3. lion
4. add
5. now
6. pie

Page 206

Top
1. shake
2. excited
3. bump
4. wonderful
5. library
6. wheel

Bottom
1. sun
2. dish
3. foot
4. horn
5. ten
6. fox

Page 207

Top
ice, mittens
sled, skate
snow, cold

Bottom
table
telephone
room, chair
oven, bathtub

Page 208

Top
1. angry
2. proud
3. sad
4. sorry
5. glad
6. afraid

Bottom
1. hammer
2. shovel
3. screwdriver
4. rake
5. broom
6. saw

Page 209

Down
1. ground
2. note
3. inside

Across
2. neighbor
4. bounce
5. ladder

Page 210

Down
1. straight
2. people

Across
3. teacher
4. slide
5. high
6. teeth

Page 211

Top
1. deer
2. nose
3. pear
4. see
5. tale
6. through

Bottom
1. deer
2. tail
3. nose
4. sea
5. through
6. pairs

Page 212

Top
1. hole
2. hi
3. ant
4. clothes
5. knight
6. ate

Bottom
1. eight
2. Close
3. aunt
4. whole
5. night
6. high

Page 213

Top
E
B
C
A
F
D

Bottom
pen – well

Page 214

Top
B
D
E
C
F
A

Bottom
track – foot

Page 215

Top
A
F
D
C
B
E

Bottom
pop – giant

Page 216

Top
D
C
B
E
F
A

Bottom
letter – basket

Page 217

1. gopher
2. hogan
3. gear
4. dormouse
5. outrigger
6. harp

Page 218

1. lynx
2. quiver
3. milestone
4. poncho
5. manager
6. fisher

Page 219

1. locked
2. spaceship
3. pounding
4. planet
5. robot
6. noise

Page 220

1. sleep
2. blanket
3. warm
4. ago
5. leather
6. leaves

Page 221

1. oven
2. pick
3. dough
4. heap
5. berries
6. pie

Page 222

1. square
2. pentagon
3. triangle
4. rectangle
5. hexagon
6. diamond

The **long o** sound can be spelled **oa**, as in **boat**.
Draw a box around each word that has the **long o** sound.

1. I want a roast beef sandwich, please.

2. Todd wore a heavy coat as he walked down the road.

3. Who put this jelly on my toast?

4. The goat looked at the toad.

5. Will kicked the football over the goal.

6. A boat will float.

Spell the words to see the difference a letter makes.

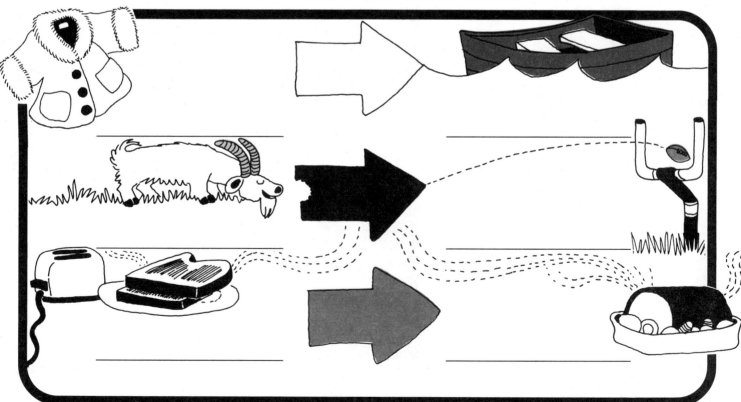

The **long a** sound can be spelled **ai**, as in **mail**.
Spell the words by adding the **long a** sound to each.

1. You think with this.   b r ___ ___ n

2. You walk on this in the woods.   t r ___ ___ l

3. Water runs down it.   d r ___ ___ n

4. It runs on a track.   t r ___ ___ n

5. This animal moves very slowly.   s n ___ ___ l

6. Another word for bucket is ____.   p ___ ___ l

Spell the words to see the difference a letter makes.

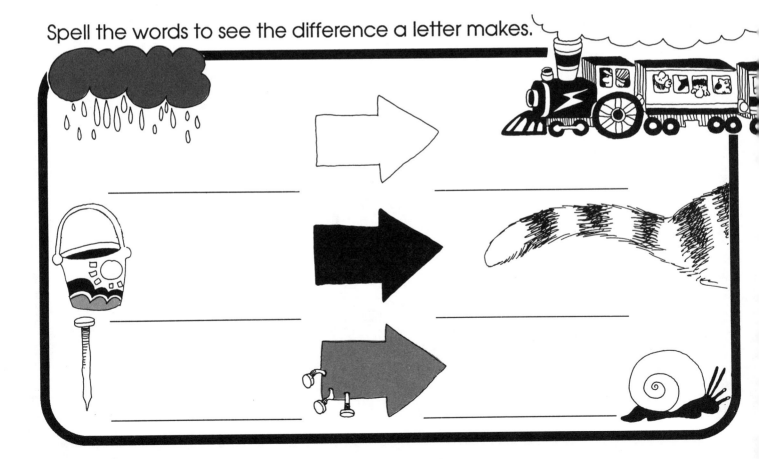

The **long e** sound can be spelled **ee**, as in **see**.
Write each **long e** word under its picture.

bee	teepee	sheep	tree	jeep	queen

_____   _____   _____

_____   _____   _____

Spell the **long e** words.
Then read the story out loud.

Oh, no! I **s** ___ ___ a **b** ___ ___ in a **t r** ___ ___ and it is
after me.   It is time to **f l** ___ ___ ! Oh, my. I cannot
k ___ ___ **p** up this **s p** ___ ___ **d**. I **f** ___ ___ **l** I am slowing
down. I must not **w** ___ ___ **p**. I know! I'll hide by this
w ___ ___ **d**. Ha! The **b** ___ ___ does not....Ouch!

The long **e** sound can be spelled **ea**, as in **mean**.
Use the letters to spell six **long e** words.

t s a j e b m l n f

_____   _____

_____   _____

_____   _____

Read each sentence. Circle the word that is spelled wrong.
Spell the word correctly on the line.

1. We saw a rele rabbit.   _____

2. Sue is strong, not wek.   _____

3. I can rede a book.   _____

4. Jody loves to ete pizza.   _____

5. Please clean your room so that it is nete. _____

6. The giant ate a bowl of green bens.   _____

The **long a** sound can be spelled **ay**, as in **say**.
Write each **long a** word under its picture.

hay   tray   spray   pay   jay   play

Read each riddle.
Spell the **long a** answer.

I rhyme with **play**.
You use me to make things.
I am soft and easy to mold.

I am _____ .

I rhyme with **pay**.
I am the fifth month.

I am _____ .

I rhyme with **day**.
I am a color.
Clouds with rain look like me.

I am _____ .

I rhyme with **hay**.
I am the opposite of night.

I am _____ .

The **long a** sound can be spelled **a __ e**, as in **cake**, **same**, **race**.
Draw a box around each word that has the **long a** sound.

1. Tim put the flowers in a yellow vase.

2. When the gate broke, Jane helped her father fix it.

3. The men on the crane broke a window pane.

4. Sam used a cane after he broke his foot.

5. We sat by the lake and ate cake and ice cream.

6. That ape took my tape!

Read the hints.
Then spell each **long a** word.

1. You use it to clean up leaves.   r __ __ __

2. A bear sleeps in a _____.   c __ __ __

3. Mom put the picture in a _____.   f r __ __ __

4. Kevin put the pizza on a _____.   p l __ __ __

5. Who let the parrot out of its _____?   c __ __ __

6. It's a big machine or it's a bird.   c r __ __ __

The long **i** sound can be spelled **i __ e**, as in **size**, **dime**, **ride**.
Use the letters to spell six **long i** words.

p b f i t p n k r e n

9
0

Spell the words that have a **long i** sound.

1. The color of snow is _____.   wh ___ ___ ___

2. The number after four is _____.   f ___ ___ ___

3. Whee! I won first _____.   pr ___ ___ ___

4. It belongs to me. It is _____.   m ___ ___ ___

5. Ten cents is one _____.   d ___ ___ ___

6. I like to _____ my bike.   r ___ ___ ___

The **long o** sound can be spelled **o __ e**, as in **rose**, **home**, **phone**.
Spell the **long o** words to see the difference a letter makes.

Read each riddle.
Spell the **long o** answer.

I rhyme with **cone**.
Dogs chew on me.

I am a _____.

I rhyme with **pole**.
You dig me.

I am a _____.

I rhyme with **dome**.
I am where you live.

I am _____.

I rhyme with **woke**.
I am funny.

I am a _____.

The letters **st**, **sp**, and **sw** can be used to begin words.
Draw a box around each word that starts with **st**, **sp**, or **sw**.

1. Jill needs a stamp for her letter.

2. The swan swam away.

3. The spider sat on the stove.

4. I like to eat sweet stuff with a spoon.

5. It's his turn to swing.

6. Start the speedy sports car race.

Spell the words.

The letters **spr**, **scr**, and **str** can be used to begin words.
Write each word under its picture.

screw   strike   spray   strong   scratch   spring

Spell the words that start with **spr**, **str**, or **scr**.
Then read the story out loud.

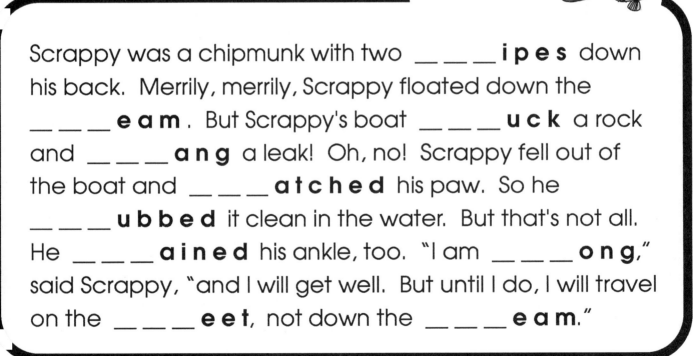

Scrappy was a chipmunk with two __ __ __ **i p e s** down
his back. Merrily, merrily, Scrappy floated down the
__ __ __ **e a m**. But Scrappy's boat __ __ __ **u c k** a rock
and __ __ __ **a n g** a leak! Oh, no! Scrappy fell out of
the boat and __ __ __ **a t c h e d** his paw. So he
__ __ __ **u b b e d** it clean in the water. But that's not all.
He __ __ __ **a i n e d** his ankle, too. "I am __ __ __ **o n g**,"
said Scrappy, "and I will get well. But until I do, I will travel
on the __ __ __ **e e t**, not down the __ __ __ **e a m**."

The **short a** sound can be spelled **a**, as in **apple**.
Draw a box around each word that has the **short a** sound.

1. I rubbed the apple on my pants.

2. Amy hurt her hand, so she could not clap.

3. Your bike will be flat if you leave it on the tracks!

4. Alan likes to wear pants with blue stripes.

5. Please move the mouse trap back.

6. The man read the road map.

Spell the **short a** words.

_____   _____

_____   _____

_____   _____

235

The **short i** sound can be spelled **i**, as in **it**.
Spell the **short i** words.

1. It's magic! It's a _____.   __ __ __ c k

2. It's white and you drink it.   __ __ l k

3. You wear it on your finger.   __ __ n g

4. I will not lose. I will _____.   w __ __

5. A lion tamer uses a _____.   w h __ __

6. You do this to a baseball.   __ __ t

Write each **short i** word under its picture.

| lift | trip | mix | middle | fill | little |

_____   _____   _____

_____   _____   _____

The **short u** sound can be spelled **u**, as in **bug**.
Write each **short u** word under its picture.

bus   jug   truck   drum   rug   duck

_____   _____   _____

_____   _____   _____

Read each riddle.
Spell the **short u** answer.

It rhymes with **hut**.
You do it with a knife.

The word is _____.

It rhymes with **bunny**.
It makes you laugh.

It is very _____.

It rhymes with **jump**.
Camels have one or two.

The word is _____.

It rhymes with **mutter**.
You put it on bread.

It is _____.

The **short o** sound can be spelled **o**, as in **top**.
Spell the **short o** words.

1. A red traffic light means _____.   s t __ __

2. It tells you the time.   __ __ __ c k

3. The turtle sat on a _____.   r __ __ __

4. Don't _____ that ball!   d r __ __

5. You use it on a door for safety.   l __ __ __

6. The baby has the _____.   b l __ __ __

Use the letters to spell six **short o** words.

c   o   b   l   k   s   x   p   c   m

_____   _____

_____

_____   _____

238

The **short e** sound can be spelled **e**, as in **let** and **when**.
Draw a box around each word that has the **short e** sound.

1. When will I get a new dress?

2. Help me put this box on the desk, please.

3. Ben loves jelly on his toast.

4. I will spend my penny.

5. Jenny ran up the steps.

6. We slept in a tent last night.

Look at the picture.
Spell the **short e** word for each picture.

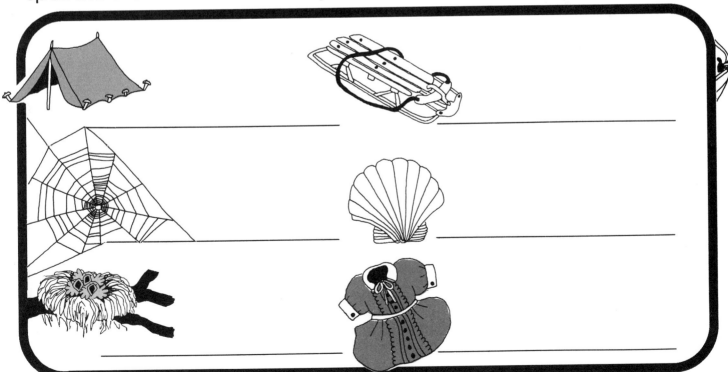

The last sounds of some words are spelled with **ch**.
And the last sounds of some words are spelled with **tch**.
Look at the words. Then write each word in the correct place.

watch   lunch   branch   witch   church   crutch

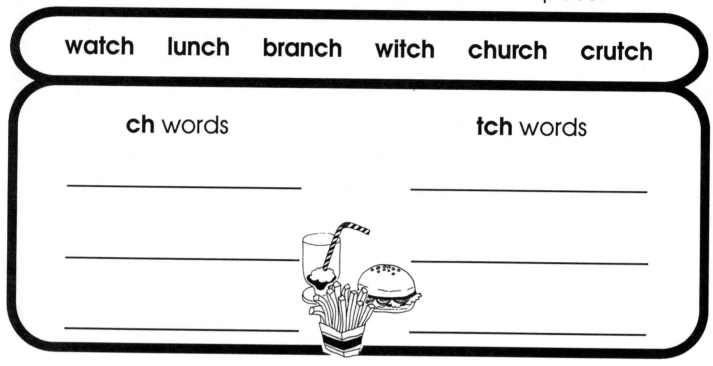

ch words   **tch** words

_____   _____

_____   _____

_____   _____

Spell the words.

The letters **th** and **wh** can be used to begin words.
Draw a box around each **th** or **wh** word.

1. Jim saw seven whales today.

2. Why don't you thank Abbie for the present?

3. My thumb hurts!

4. Where is the wheel?

5. Mrs. Parton uses a thimble on her finger.

6. Which thorn tore my pants?

Use the letters to spell six words.

w t h e l i p r u y e m b a

_____

_____

_____

_____

The letter **r** changes some sounds.
It changes the sound of **a** and **o** when it comes after them.
Say each **r-word** out loud. Then spell it under the correct picture.

farm	dart	horn	star	shark	fort

_____   _____   _____

_____   _____   _____

Spell the words.

1. It's the opposite of **long**.   __ __ o r __

2. You buy things in it.   s t __ __ e

3. You eat with one.   __ o r __

4. It's the opposite of **dumb**.   __ __ a r __

5. It's the opposite of **finish** .   __ __ __ __ t

6. It's the opposite of **light**.   d __ __ __

MOM & POP

The letter **r** changes some sounds.
It changes the sound of **e**, **i**, and **u** when it comes after them.
Say each **r-word** out loud. Then spell it under the correct picture.

turkey   girl   tiger   surf   circus   mother

Read each riddle.
Spell the **r-word** answer.

I rhyme with **maker**.
I cook all day —
cookies, cakes, and pies.

I am a _____.

I rhyme with **shirt**.
I am clothes like pants,
but without legs.

I am a _____.

I rhyme with **turn**.
You get me if you stay
too long in the sun.

I am a _____.

I rhyme with **purse**.
I take care of you
if you are sick.

I am a _____.

Listen to the vowel sound in **boy**.
Sometimes that sound is spelled **oy**, and sometimes it is spelled **oi**.
Read the sentences below. Circle the words with this vowel sound.

1. To be happy is to be full of joy.

2. The cats and dogs were making a lot of noise.

3. Please do not point at that toy.

4. Gretchen planted the seeds in soil.

5. That color is called royal blue.

6. Joyce and Roy are my friends.

Spell the words.

1. It means to make water very, very hot.　　**b __ __ l**

2. A dime is one. So is a penny.　　**c __ __ __**

3. To have fun is to_____.　　**e n __ __ __**

4. To become part of a group is to _____.　　**j __ __ __**

5. Loud sounds are _____.　　**__ __ __ s e**

6. When you sing, you use your _____.　　**__ __ __ c e**

244

Listen to the vowel sound in **moon**.
That sound can be spelled **oo**.
Use the letters to spell six words.

s m g z o r t p n o t e h b

Read each riddle.
Spell the answer.

I rhyme with **moo**.
You come to see
animals here.

I am a _____.

I rhyme with **cool**.
You swim in me.

I am a _____.

I rhyme with **moon**.
I am a time.

I am _____.

I rhyme with **toot**.
You wear me like a shoe.

I am a _____.

Listen to the vowel sound in **cook**.
That sound can be spelled **oo**.
Spell the **oo** words below.

1. To see something, you _____.   l __ __ __

2. A small river is a _____.   b r __ __ __

3. You catch fish with one.   __ __ __ k

4. You have one at the end of your leg.   __ o o __

5. We get it from sheep.   __ __ __ l

6. You make a fire with it.   __ __ __ d

Spell the **oo** words. Then read the story out loud.

Mom likes to **c** __ __ **k**. She has a new **c** __ __ **k** __ __ __ **k**.
Today, she gave me a __ __ __ **k i e** to eat before I went
out to play. Yum. It was **g** __ __ __. It is cold out, so I
t __ __ __ my warm jacket. Brr! I put on the jacket right
away. And I put up its **h** __ __ **d**. Then I just **s t** __ __ __
there. Snow fell on me, but I **s h** __ __ __ it off. Lisa came
by. "Let's go down to the **b r** __ __ __," she said. So we did.

The **long o** sound can be spelled **ow**, as in **slow**.
Read the sentences below.
Draw a box around each word in which **long o** is spelled **ow**.

1. "Do not throw the dish," said the rabbit.

2. The bear slept in the snow.

3. Did the bear use a pillow?

4. Oh-oh. What is making that big shadow?

5. Tim saw the rainbow before I did.

6. A crow flew into the window!

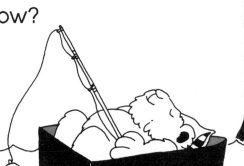

Read each sentence. Circle the word that is spelled wrong.
Spell the word correctly on the line.

1. Each year I groe taller.   _____

2. This balloon was hard to blo up.   _____

3. Kyle is fast, not sloe.   _____

4. Jason can throo the ball far.   _____

5. Please sho me the way home.   _____

6. That color is yello.   _____

Listen to the vowel sound in **cow**.
Sometimes that sound is spelled **ow**, and sometimes it is spelled **ou**.
Look at the words. Then write each word in the correct place.

ground	brown	bounce	owl	shower	count

ow words  **ou** words

_____   _____

_____   _____

_____   _____

Spell the words.

_____   _____

_____   _____

_____   _____

Listen to the vowel sound in **saw**.
Sometimes that sound is spelled **aw**, and sometimes it is spelled **au**.
Look at the words. Then write each word in the correct place.

| draw | auto | haul | yawn | hawk | because |

aw words   **au** words

_____   _____

_____   _____

_____   _____

Read each riddle.
Spell the answer.

It rhymes with **draw**.
Cows and horses sleep on it.

The word is _____.

It rhymes with **haul**.
It's a boy's name.

The word is _____.

It rhymes with **taught**.
It is the past of catch.

The word is _____.

It rhymes with **law**.
It moves when you chew.

The word is _____.

The **long e** sound can be spelled **y**, as in **candy**.
Read the sentences below.
Draw a box around each word in which **long e** is spelled **y**.

1. "It's berry jelly," said the chimp.

2. See a penny, pick it up.

3. Do you eat candy?

4. The puppy looked at the baby.

5. My dog is furry and very pretty.

6. Sara ate one cherry and one strawberry.

Spell the words.

_____   _____

_____   _____

_____   _____

How do you spell the word for more than one?
For most words, you just add an **s**, as in **beds**, **cows**, **plants**.
Spell the word for each picture below.

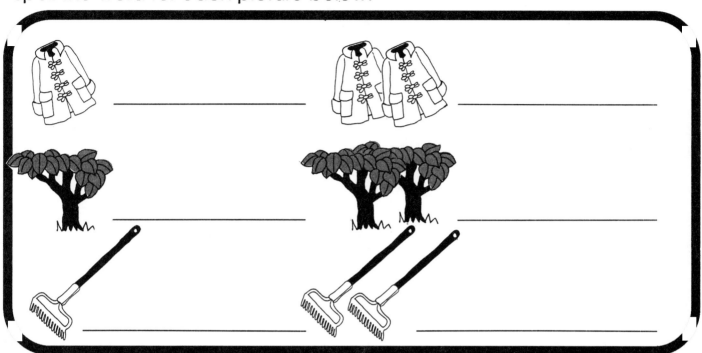

Spell each word for more than one.

more than one **lamp** _____

more than one **apple** _____

more than one **tiger** _____

more than one **bird** _____

more than one **frog** _____

more than one **kite** _____

How do you spell the word for more than one?
If a word ends in **x** or **ss**, you add **es,** as in **foxes** or **glasses**.
Spell the word for each picture below.

_____   _____

_____   _____

_____   _____

Spell each word for more than one.

more than one **kiss**   _____

more than one **ax**   _____

more than one **duck**   _____

more than one **cross**   _____

more than one **fox**   _____

more than one **mailbox**   _____

How do you spell the word for more than one?
If a word ends in **ch** or **sh**, you add **es,** as in **benches** or **wishes**.
Spell the word for each picture below.

_____   _____

_____   _____

_____   _____

Spell each word for more than one.

more than one **nail**   _____

more than one **ranch**   _____

more than one **watch**   _____

more than one **farmer**   _____

more than one **dish**   _____

more than one **bush**   _____

Usually, if a word ends in **y**, you change the **y** to **i** and add **es**.
The word for more than one bunny is **bunnies**.
Spell the word for each picture below.

Spell each word for more than one.

more than one **berry**   _____

more than one **story**   _____

more than one **princess**   _____

more than one **fly**   _____

more than one **city**   _____

more than one **spot**   _____

Page 225
Top
1. roast
2. coat, road
3. toast
4. goat, toad
5. goal
6. boat, float

Bottom
coat, boat
goat, goal
toast, roast

Page 226
Top
1. brain
2. trail
3. drain
4. train
5. snail
6. pail

Bottom
rain, train
pail, tail
nail, snail

Page 227
Top
sheep, queen, teepee
bee, jeep, tree

Bottom
see, bee, tree
flee
keep, speed, feel
weep
weed, bee

Page 228
Top
seal, team
bean, leaf
meat, jeans

Bottom
1. rele – real
2. wek – weak
3. rede – read
4. ete – eat
5. nete – neat
6. bens – beans

Page 229
Top
jay, play, pay
tray, spray, hay

Bottom
clay, May
gray, day

Page 230
Top
1. vase
2. gate, Jane
3. crane, pane
4. cane
5. lake, ate, cake
6. ape, tape

Bottom
1. rake
2. cave
3. frame
4. plate
5. cage
6. crane

Page 231
Top
bike, nine
kite, tire
fire, pipe

Bottom
1. white
2. five
3. prize
4. mine
5. dime
6. ride

Page 232
Top
rope, robe
nose, hose
bone, cone

Bottom
bone, hole
home, joke

Page 233
Top
1. stamp
2. swan, swam
3. spider, stove
4. sweet, stuff, spoon
5. swing
6. start, speedy, sports

Bottom
swing, swan
spider, spoon
stove, stamp

Page 234
Top
scratch, strike, strong
screw, spring, spray

Bottom
stripes
stream, struck
sprang
scratched
scrubbed
sprained, strong
street, stream

Page 235
Top
1. apple, pants
2. hand, clap
3. flat, tracks
4. Alan, pants
5. trap, back
6. man, map

Bottom
ants, apple
trap, tracks
ham, band

Page 236
Top
1. trick
2. milk
3. ring
4. win
5. whip
6. hit

Bottom
fill, middle, trip
lift, little, mix

Page 237
Top
bus, drum, jug
duck, rug, truck

Bottom
cut, funny
hump, butter

Page 238
Top
1. stop
2. clock
3. rock
4. drop
5. lock
6. block

Bottom
lock, block
box, sock
clock, mop

Page 239
Top
1. When, get, dress
2. Help, desk
3. Ben, jelly
4. spend, penny
5. Jenny, steps
6. slept, tent

Bottom
tent, sled
web, shell
nest, dress

Page 240

Top

ch   tch
lunch   watch
branch   witch
church   crutch

Bottom
watch, church
witch, bench
branch, crutch

Page 241

Top
1. whales
2. Why, thank
3. thumb
4. Where, wheel
5. thimble
6. Which, thorn

Bottom
whale, thumb
thirty, whip
wheel, thimble

Page 242

Top
horn, farm, fort
dart, star, shark

Bottom
1. short
2. store
3. fork
4. smart
5. start
6. dark

Page 243

Top
mother, surf, tiger
turkey, girl, circus

Bottom
baker, skirt
burn, nurse

Page 244

Top
1. joy
2. noise
3. point, toy
4. soil
5. royal
6. Joyce, Roy

Bottom
1. boil
2. coin
3. enjoy
4. join
5. noise
6. voice

Page 245

Top
broom, moon
spoon, tooth
zoo, goose

Bottom
zoo, pool
noon, boot

Page 246

Top
1. look
2. brook
3. hook
4. foot
5. wool
6. wood

Bottom
cook, cookbook
cookie
good
took
hood, stood
shook
brook

Page 247

Top
1. throw
2. snow
3. pillow
4. shadow
5. rainbow
6. crow, window

Bottom
1. groe – grow
2. blo – blow
3. sloe – slow
4. throo – throw
5. sho – show
6. yello – yellow

Page 248

Top

ow   ou
brown   ground
owl   bounce
shower count

Bottom
cloud, crown
clown, mouse
house, flower

Page 249

Top

aw   au
draw   auto
yawn   haul
hawk   because

Bottom
straw, Paul, Saul
caught, jaw

Page 250

Top
1. berry, jelly
2. penny
3. candy
4. puppy, baby
5. furry, very, pretty
6. cherry, strawberry

Bottom
penny, cherry
strawberry, puppy
jelly, candy

Page 251

Top
coat, coats
tree, trees
rake, rakes

Bottom
lamps
apples
tigers
birds
frogs
kites

Page 252

Top
fox, foxes
dress, dresses
box, boxes

Bottom
kisses
axes
ducks
crosses
foxes
mailboxes

Page 253

Top
brush, brushes
witch, witches
bench, benches

Bottom
nails
ranches
watches
farmers
dishes
bushes

Page 254

Top
puppy, puppies
penny, pennies
baby, babies

Bottom
berries
stories
princesses
flies
cities
spots

Naming words name animals, people, things, or places.
Duck, nurse, forks, and **home** are **naming words**.
Circle the 12 **naming words** below.

aunt   meet   happy   apartment   nice   tents

most   deep   bottles   chickens   even   loud

jump   bake   bridge   telephone   river   sheep

clean   uncle   bright   doctors   monkey   knew

Look at the **naming words** you circled.
Write a **naming word** in each sentence below.

1. I like _____ .

2. Three _____ ran away.

3. My _____ is nice.

4. Jason painted the_____ red.

Circle each **naming word**.

1. My (grandmother) sent me a (letter)

2. The crows like to eat our corn.

3. The boy has seven sisters.

4. Is the giant friendly?

5. The dragon drank the river dry.

Circle each **naming word**.

1. The farmer broke the eggs.

2. That monkey likes bananas.

3. The wolf carried a basket.

4. The doctor answered the telephone.

5. The teacher blew a whistle.

258

Some **naming words** name special animals, people, or places.
These **naming words** start with a capital letter.
Write the **naming words** in correct pairs.

boy
Jumbo
Julie
Derek
New York
girl
elephant
city

NAMING WORD	SPECIAL NAMING WORD
1. boy	Derek
2. _____	_____
3. _____	_____
4. _____	_____

Write the **naming words** in correct pairs.

man
Texas
woman
Mickey
state
dog
Beth
mouse
Mr. Jones
Lassie

NAMING WORD	SPECIAL NAMING WORD
1. _____	_____
2. _____	_____
3. _____	_____
4. _____	_____
5. _____	_____

Circle only the **special naming words**.

1. Beth, Bryan, and Brenda are triplets.

2. His uncle lives in Texas.

3. My mules are named Mistake and Trouble.

4. We like the red Ford car.

5. My dog, Dusty, digs holes in the garden.

Circle only the **special naming words**.

1. Our cat is named Jinks.

2. Rosa told a story to Luis.

3. We drove from Vermont to Florida.

4. Robin has a horse named Mo.

5. Yes, I have a pair of Nike shoes.

Some words can take the place of a **naming word**.
He, **she**, **them**, and **us** can take the place of a **naming word**.
Write the word that can take the place of the underlined words.

they

it

she

he

1. <u>Danny</u> counted the stars. _He_

2. Melissa ate <u>the cake</u>. _____

3. <u>Your friends</u> are here. _____

4. <u>Anne</u> found the lost lamb. _____

5. <u>My brother</u> walked all day long. _____

Write the word that can take the place of the underlined words.

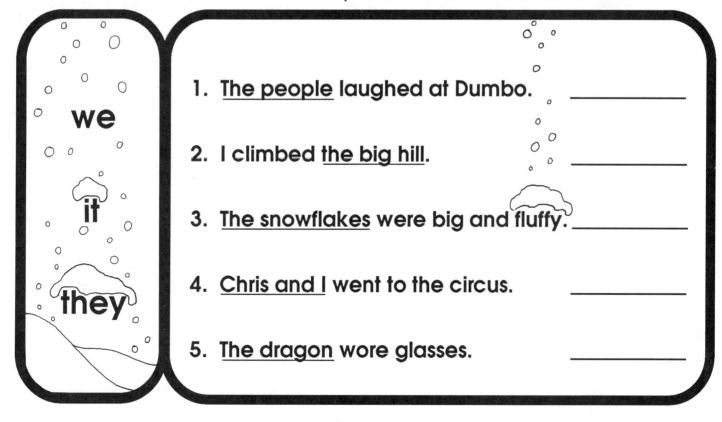

we

it

they

1. <u>The people</u> laughed at Dumbo. _____

2. I climbed <u>the big hill</u>. _____

3. <u>The snowflakes</u> were big and fluffy. _____

4. <u>Chris and I</u> went to the circus. _____

5. <u>The dragon</u> wore glasses. _____

Write the word that can take the place of the underlined words.

her

him

them

1. Give the honey to <u>the bears</u> now. _____

2. Hold the ladder for <u>Jon</u>, please. _____

3. The lion listened to <u>Sheila</u>. _____

4. I asked <u>Ken</u> a hard question. _____

5. The tiger frightened <u>the people</u>. _____

Write the word that can take the place of the underlined words.

us

them

1. I gave the book to <u>Dan and Lee</u>. _____

2. Mom made a pie for <u>my aunt and me</u>. _____

3. The snowflakes fell on <u>Jack and me</u>. _____

4. Who saw <u>the doctors</u>? _____

5. I play with <u>Tom, Sally, and Fred</u>. _____

Write **'s** after a name to show that something belongs to it.
Emily's umbrella was under **Kevin's coat**.
Write the **naming word** correctly on each line.

Susan   1. That is _____Susan's_____ breakfast.

Rascal   2. Don't touch _____ ball!

Chad   3. _____ jacket doesn't fit me.

Zipper   4. _____ puppies are cute.

Lori   5. The jeep roared through _____ garden.

Write the **naming word** correctly on each line.

Lin   1. I like _____ sister.

Paul   2. We rode on _____ boat.

Mudpie   3. _____ bowl was empty.

Superman   4. Don't pull on _____ cape.

Ting   5. Mr. _____ flowers won first prize.

Write **'s** after a name to show that something belongs to it.
Emily's umbrella was under **Kevin's coat**.
Write the **naming word** correctly on each line.

Ryan   1. _____ mother gave us ice cream.

Hogan   2. Shh! This is _____ hideout.

Gail   3. _____ goose chased me.

Lucky   4. Leave _____ bone alone!

Richard   5. Did _____ magic tricks make you happy?

Write the **naming word** correctly on each line.

Hogan   1. I followed _____ footprints.

Max   2. You can wear _____ big coat.

Weston   3. Mrs. _____ car stopped.

Batman   4. This looks like _____ mask.

Yoko   5. _____ father is our teacher.

264

A **telling sentence** begins with a capital and ends with a period.
Write a **telling sentence** for each set of words.

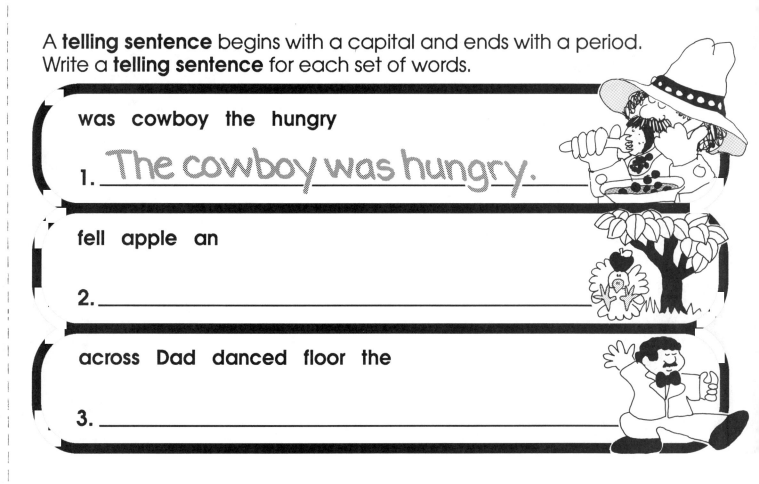

was   cowboy   the   hungry

1. _The cowboy was hungry._

fell   apple   an

2. _____

across   Dad   danced   floor   the

3. _____

A **telling sentence** begins with a capital and ends with a period.
Write a **telling sentence** for each set of words.

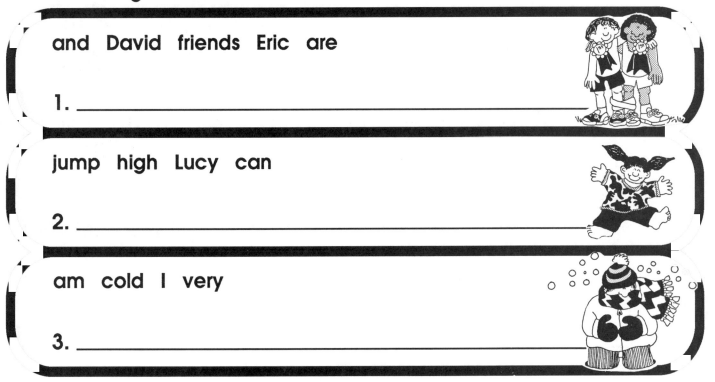

and   David   friends   Eric   are

1. _____

jump   high   Lucy   can

2. _____

am   cold   I   very

3. _____

A **telling sentence** begins with a capital and ends with a period.
Write a **telling sentence** for each set of words.

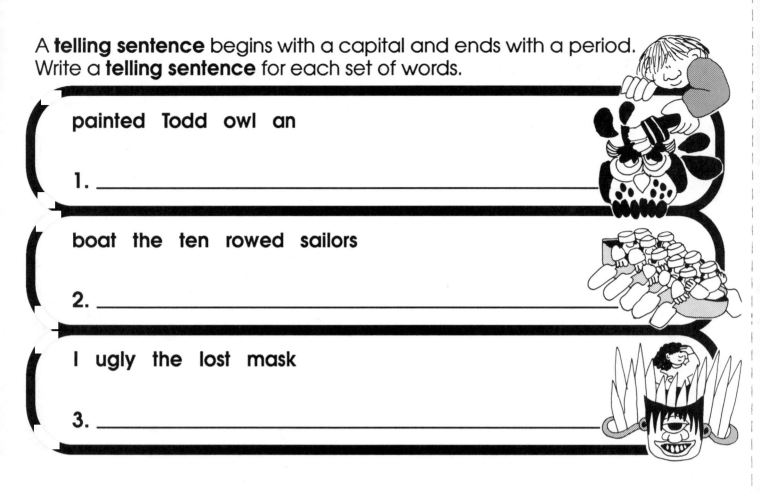

painted Todd owl an

1. _____

boat the ten rowed sailors

2. _____

I ugly the lost mask

3. _____

A **telling sentence** begins with a capital and ends with a period.
Write a **telling sentence** for each set of words.

Walter first was here

1. _____

bear sleep the to went

2. _____

best he my is friend

3. _____

266

An **asking sentence** begins with a capital and ends with a question mark.
Write an **asking sentence** for each set of words.

skate this Amy's is

1. _Is this Amy's skate?_

took who monkey Michael's

2. _____

does soccer play Cheryl

3. _____

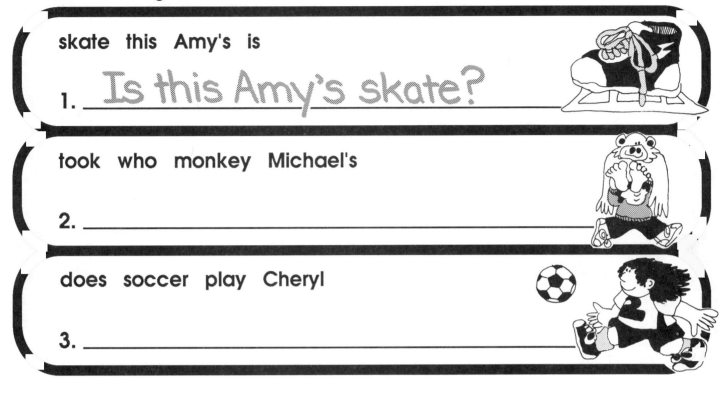

An **asking sentence** begins with a capital and ends with a question mark.
Write an **asking sentence** for each set of words.

has my who lunch

1. _____

you game the going are to

2. _____

Scott kick did the ball

3. _____

An **asking sentence** begins with a capital and ends with a question mark. Write an **asking sentence** for each set of words.

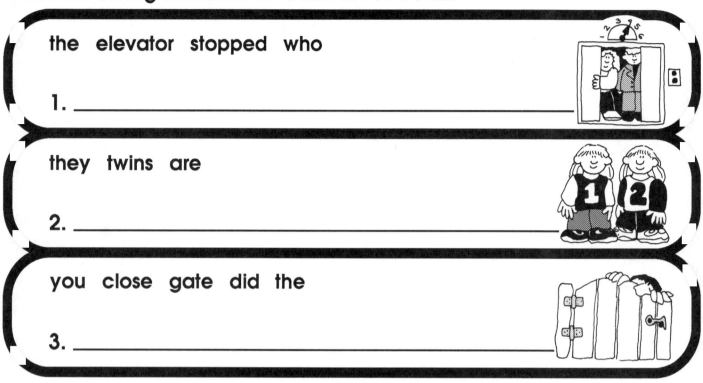

the   elevator   stopped   who

1. _____

they   twins   are

2. _____

you   close   gate   did   the

3. _____

An **asking sentence** begins with a capital and ends with a question mark. Write an **asking sentence** for each set of words.

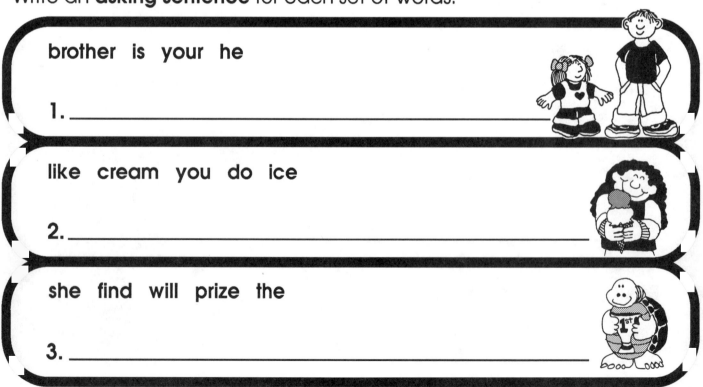

brother   is   your   he

1. _____

like   cream   you   do   ice

2. _____

she   find   will   prize   the

3. _____

Action words tell what somebody is doing or what is happening.
Hop, ask, and **see** are **action words.**
Circle the 12 **action words** below.

glass	add	people	snowman	grow	dig
feed	his	roof	careful	smile	pink
meet	tail	crawl	numbers	reach	song
shout	pay	table	yellow	drive	love

Look at the **action words** you circled.
Write an **action word** in each sentence below.

1. Please _____ the dog.

2. Can you _____ ?

3. I like to _____ .

4. Did you _____ that man?

Circle every **action word**.

1. Debbie (slid) and Sean (tripped).

2. Six ducks quacked and splashed.

3. Who stretched my sleeves?

4. Fred milked the cows and fed the pigs.

5. I carry the ice cream.

Circle every **action word**.

1. The teacher blew a whistle.

2. I buy apples.

3. The rabbit hops and the bear runs.

4. I blew out the candles and cut the cake.

5. An elephant sat in the pool.

Action words tell what happens now or what happened in the past.
Eric **plays** tells about now. Eric **played** tells about the past.
Write the **action words** in correct pairs.

learn		NOW	PAST
followed			
hop		1. _learn_	_learned_
licked			
lick		2. _____	_____
follow			
hopped		3. _____	_____
learned		4. _____	_____

Write the **action words** in correct pairs.

live		NOW	PAST
asked			
work		1. _____	_____
picked			
lived		2. _____	_____
worked			
use		3. _____	_____
ask			
pick		4. _____	_____
used		5. _____	_____

Write the **action words** in correct pairs.

eat
drink
flew
run
ate
fly
thought
think
drank
ran

NOW	PAST
1. _____	_____
2. _____	_____
3. _____	_____
4. _____	_____
5. _____	_____

Write the **action words** in correct pairs.

find
sang
ride
did
sing
know
found
do
knew
rode

NOW	PAST
1. _____	_____
2. _____	_____
3. _____	_____
4. _____	_____
5. _____	_____

272

Some **action words** can be written in special ways.
Do + not can be written **don't**.
Draw a line between the words that mean the same thing.

1. are not   isn't

2. is not   didn't

3. has not   couldn't

4. could not   aren't

5. did not   hasn't

Draw a line between the words that mean the same thing.

1. can not   doesn't

2. were not   won't

3. was not   can't

4. will not   wasn't

5. does not   weren't

What does each **action word** mean?
Write the words on each line.

1. isn't = _____is_____ _____not_____

2. hasn't = _____ _____

3. didn't = _____ _____

4. couldn't = _____ _____

5. aren't = _____ _____

6. doesn't = _____ _____

7. can't = _____ _____

8. won't = _____ _____

9. weren't = _____ _____

10. wouldn't = _____ _____

11. haven't = _____ _____

12. wasn't = _____ _____

Write an **asking sentence** or a **telling sentence** for each set of words. Begin and end each sentence correctly.

beans the didn't I spill

1. _____

last who laughed

2. _____

horn Hugo the huge held

3. _____

Write an **asking sentence** or a **telling sentence** for each set of words. Begin and end each sentence correctly.

wash socks please my

1. _____

jump how high Lucy can

2. _____

three the saw Goldilocks bears

3. _____

Write an **asking sentence** or a **telling sentence** for each set of words. Begin and end each sentence correctly.

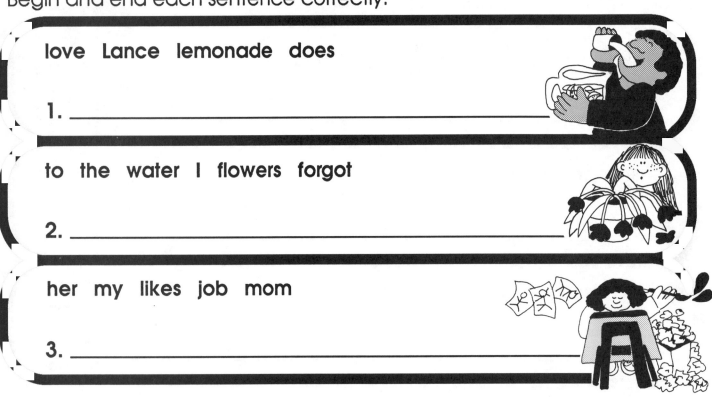

love Lance lemonade does

1. _____

to the water I flowers forgot

2. _____

her my likes job mom

3. _____

Write an **asking sentence** or a **telling sentence** for each set of words. Begin and end each sentence correctly.

did fox away run the

1. _____

nest the eggs full was of

2. _____

you are here why

3. _____

276

Write an **asking sentence** or a **telling sentence** for each set of words. Begin and end each sentence correctly.

unhappy cried twice the twins

1. _____

she bike leave her did outside

2. _____

thumb today my hurts

3. _____

Write an **asking sentence** or a **telling sentence** for each set of words. Begin and end each sentence correctly.

Alan fast sure walks

1. _____

red leaves yellow were and the

2. _____

tiger that think sad is I

3. _____

Write an **asking sentence** or a **telling sentence** for each set of words. Begin and end each sentence correctly.

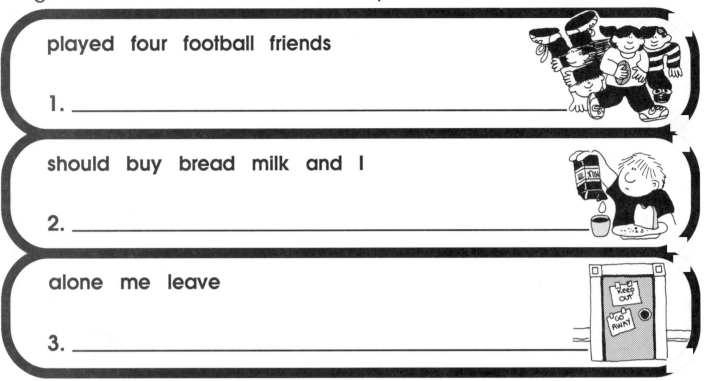

played four football friends

1. _____

should buy bread milk and I

2. _____

alone me leave

3. _____

Write an **asking sentence** or a **telling sentence** for each set of words. Begin and end each sentence correctly.

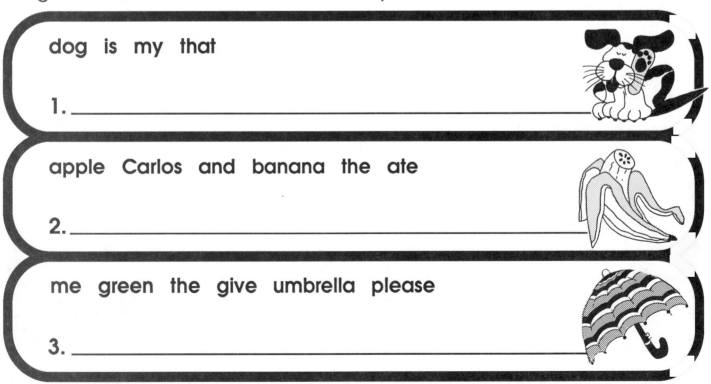

dog is my that

1. _____

apple Carlos and banana the ate

2. _____

me green the give umbrella please

3. _____

Words that tell colors or numbers are **describing words**.
Words that tell how things sound, look, or feel are also **describing words**.
Blue, seven, loud, pretty, and **sad** are **describing words**.
Circle every **describing word** below.

1. The (young) (spotted) horse loved the (old) (brown) dog.

2. Benjamin painted a wonderful picture.

3. Listen to the twelve noisy pigs!

4. Here are your clean shirts and dirty shoes.

5. The short man danced with the tall woman.

Circle every **describing word** below.

1. Rosa told Luis a funny story.

2. The green and yellow dragon looked at me.

3. Ten trucks made a terrible noise.

4. A smart raccoon chased the red fox.

5. Jill wore rubber boots and a wool hat.

Circle every **describing word** below.

1. This is my soft, yellow sweater.

2. Seven sad seals swam in the warm water.

3. The bald man looked at the flat tire.

4. Katherine drank a huge glass of delicious milk.

5. Two brave women chased the fat robber.

Circle every **describing word** below.

1. Jinks, our lazy cat, would not chase the fat mouse.

2. The hungry lion looked at the birthday cake.

3. Three good goats ate the garbage.

4. Roger has five dollars and twelve cents.

5. Wilma won first prize.

Some **describing words** are used to compare things.
Tall, **taller**, and **tallest** can be used to compare things.
Write in the missing words on each line.

1. ___cold___   ___colder___   ___coldest___

2. ___deep___   _____   _____

3. _____   ___braver___   _____

4. _____   _____   ___softest___

5. ___clean___   _____   _____

Write in the missing words on each line.

1. _____   ___bigger___   _____

2. ___loud___   _____   _____

3. _____   _____   ___smartest___

4. ___proud___   _____   _____

5. _____   ___newer___   _____

First read all three sentences in each box.
Then write the correct word on each line.

strong   **stronger**   **strongest**

1. Bruno is a _____ man.

2. He is the _____ man in the world.

3. But he is not _____ than Mighty Marie.

large   **largest**   **largest**

1. Who wants the _____ piece of cake?

2. My piece is _____ than your piece.

3. Gregory doesn't want a _____ piece of cake.

First read all three sentences in each box.
Then write the correct word on each line.

dark   **darker**   **darkest**

1. It's even _____ when we go to sleep.

2. Sometimes it is _____ when we come home from school.

3. But the middle of the night is the _____ time of all.

high   **higher**   **highest**

1. Mike stood on the roof. He was even _____.

2. Kelly stood on a tall mountain. He was _____.

3. Cathy stood on a ladder. She was _____.

Some words tell **where**, **when**, or **how**.
There and **outside** tell **where**.
Circle the words that tell **where**.

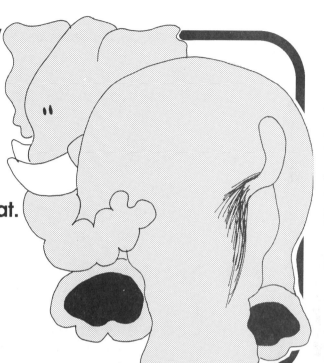

1. Kai and Elizabeth played indoors.

2. The elephant walked away.

3. Here is the dog, and there is the cat.

4. We are going outdoors.

5. Walter! Come here!

Circle the words that tell **where**.

1. The happy turtle swam around and around.

2. Here are your mittens.

3. The bear climbed up, but it would not climb down.

4. At last Jinks chased the mouse upstairs.

5. Ned let go of the string, and up went the balloon.

Some words tell **where**, **when**, or **how**.
Today and **then** tell **when**.
Circle the words that tell **when**.

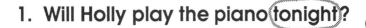

1. Will Holly play the piano (tonight)?

2. Yesterday we went to the zoo.

3. I always wash the dishes.

4. The cat ran when it saw the mice.

5. "Come visit me sometime," said the boy.

Circle the words that tell **when**.

1. Our dog never eats bones.

2. Then the hungry lion looked at me.

3. It is my birthday tomorrow.

4. "Do it now," said Dad.

5. Wilma won first prize at the fair yesterday.

284

Some words tell **where**, **when**, or **how**.
Slowly and **loudly** tell **how**.
Circle the words that tell **how**.

1. Crystal (gladly) mowed the grass.

2. Slowly the elephant walked away.

3. Edward carefully carried eleven eggs.

4. Can't you play silently?

5. Farmers work hard.

Circle the words that tell **how**.

1. I ate the ice cream happily.

2. Quickly, the mouse ran.

3. The bear stood still.

4. Gary plays the piano loudly.

5. The magician suddenly disappeared.

Some words tell **where**, **when**, or **how**.
There and **outside** tell where.
Today tells when. **Slowly** tells how.
Circle the words that tell **where**, **when**, or **how**.

1. (Then) the dragon roared and everyone ran (away).

2. Brendon never blows the bugle loudly.

3. The hunter ran upstairs, but the bear ran downstairs.

4. The monkey hid nearby.

5. Allison ate the apples yesterday.

Circle the words that tell **where**, **when**, or **how**.

1. "Will you ever learn to spell?" asked Mom.

2. Annie threw the shoes outdoors.

3. Jinks silently dragged the shoes upstairs.

4. Do you laugh when you see a cartoon?

5. Sometimes I laugh, sometimes I cry.

Page 257

Top
aunt, bottles, apartment
chickens, tents, uncle
bridge, telephone, doctors
river, monkey, sheep

Bottom
Answers will vary.

Page 258

Top
1. grandmother, letter
2. crows, corn
3. boy, sisters
4. giant
5. dragon, river

Bottom
1. farmer, eggs
2. monkey, bananas
3. wolf, basket
4. doctor, telephone
5. teacher, whistle

Page 259

Top
1. boy – Derek
2. girl – Julie
3. elephant – Jumbo
4. city – New York

Bottom
1. man – Mr. Jones
2. woman – Beth
3. state – Texas
4. dog – Lassie
5. mouse – Mickey

Page 260

Top
1. Beth, Bryan, Brenda
2. Texas
3. Mistake, Trouble
4. Ford
5. Dusty

Bottom
1. Jinks
2. Rosa, Luis
3. Vermont, Florida
4. Robin, Mo
5. Nike

Page 261

Top
1. He
2. it
3. They
4. She
5. He

Bottom
1. They
2. it
3. They
4. We
5. It

Page 262

Top
1. them
2. him
3. her
4. him
5. them

Bottom
1. them
2. us
3. us
4. them
5. them

Page 263

Top
1. Susan's
2. Rascal's
3. Chad's
4. Zipper's
5. Lori's

Bottom
1. Lin's
2. Paul's
3. Mudpie's
4. Superman's
5. Ting's

Page 264

Top
1. Ryan's
2. Hogan's
3. Gail's
4. Lucky's
5. Richard's

Bottom
1. Hogan's
2. Max's
3. Weston's
4. Batman's
5. Yoko's

Page 265

Top
1. The cowboy was hungry.
2. An apple fell.
3. Dad danced across the floor.
   Or: Across the floor Dad danced.
   Across the floor danced Dad.

Bottom
1. David and Eric are friends.
   Or: Eric and David are friends.
2. Lucy can jump high.
3. I am very cold.

Page 266

Top
1. Todd painted an owl.
   Or: An owl painted Todd.
2. Ten sailors rowed the boat.
3. I lost the ugly mask.

Bottom
1. Walter was here first.
   Or: First, Walter was here.
2. The bear went to sleep.
3. He is my best friend.

Page 267

Top
1. Is this Amy's skate?
2. Who took Michael's monkey?
3. Does Cheryl play soccer?

Bottom
1. Who has my lunch?
2. Are you going to the game?
3. Did Scott kick the ball?

Page 268

Top
1. Who stopped the elevator?
2. Are they twins?
3. Did you close the gate?

Bottom
1. Is he your brother?
2. Do you like ice cream?
3. Will she find the prize?

Page 269

Top
feed, add, grow
smile, dig, meet
pay, crawl, reach
shout, drive, love

Bottom
Answers will vary.

Page 270

Top
1. slid, tripped
2. quacked, splashed
3. stretched
4. milked, fed
5. carry

Bottom
1. blew
2. buy
3. hops, runs
4. blew, cut
5. sat

Page 271

Top
1. learn – learned
2. follow – followed
3. hop – hopped
4. lick – licked

Bottom
1. live – lived
2. ask – asked
3. work – worked
4. pick – picked
5. use – used

Page 272

Top
1. eat – ate
2. drink – drank
3. fly – flew
4. run – ran
5. think – thought

Bottom
1. find – found
2. sing – sang
3. ride – rode
4. do – did
5. know – knew

Page 273

Top
1. aren't
2. isn't
3. hasn't
4. couldn't
5. didn't

Bottom
1. can't
2. weren't
3. wasn't
4. won't
5. doesn't

Page 274

1. is not
2. has not
3. did not
4. could not
5. are not
6. does not
7. can not
8. will not
9. were not
10. would not
11. have not
12. was not

Page 275

Top
1. I didn't spill the beans.
   Or: Didn't I spill the beans?
2. Who laughed last?
3. Hugo held the huge horn.

Bottom
1. Please wash my socks.
   Or: Wash my socks, please.
2. How high can Lucy jump?
3. Goldilocks saw the three bears.
   Or: The three bears
   saw Goldilocks.

Page 278

Top
1. Four friends played football.
   Or: Four football friends played.
2. Should I buy bread and milk?
   Or: Should I buy milk and bread?
   I should buy bread and milk.
   I should buy milk and bread.
3. Leave me alone.

Bottom
1. Is that my dog?
   Or: That is my dog.
2. Carlos ate the banana and apple.
   Or: Carlos ate the apple and banana.
3. Give me the green umbrella, please.
   Or: Please give me the green umbrella.

Page 281

Top
1. cold, colder, coldest
2. deep, deeper, deepest
3. brave, braver, bravest
4. soft, softer, softest
5. clean, cleaner, cleanest

Bottom
1. big, bigger, biggest
2. loud, louder, loudest
3. smart, smarter, smartest
4. proud, prouder, proudest
5. new, newer, newest

Page 276

Top
1. Does Lance love lemonade?
   Or: Lance does love lemonade.
2. I forgot to water the flowers.
3. My mom likes her job.
   Or: Her mom likes my job.

Bottom
1. Did the fox run away?
   Or: The fox did run away.
2. The nest was full of eggs.
   Or: Was the nest full of eggs?
3. Why are you here?
   Or: Why, here you are!

Page 279

Top
1. young, spotted, old, brown
2. wonderful
3. twelve, noisy
4. clean, dirty
5. short, tall

Bottom
1. funny
2. green, yellow
3. Ten, terrible
4. smart, red
5. rubber, wool

Page 282

Top
1. Bruno is a strong man.
2. He is the strongest man in the world.
3. But he is not stronger than Mighty Marie.
1. Who wants the largest piece of cake?
2. My piece is larger than your piece.
3. Gregory doesn't want a large piece of cake.

Bottom
1. It's even darker when we go to sleep.
2. Sometimes it is dark when we come home from school.
3. But the middle of the night is the darkest time of all.
1. Mike stood on the roof. He was even higher.
2. Kelly stood on a tall mountain. He was highest.
3. Cathy stood on a ladder. She was high.

Page 277

Top
1. The unhappy twins cried twice.
   Or: Twice, the unhappy
   twins cried.
2. Did she leave her bike outside?
   Or: She did leave her
   bike outside.
3. My thumb hurts today.
   Or: Today my thumb hurts.

Bottom
1. Alan sure walks fast.
2. The leaves were red and yellow.
   Or: The leaves were yellow
   and red.
   Were the leaves red and yellow?
   Were the leaves yellow
   and red?
3. I think that tiger is sad.

Page 280

Top
1. soft, yellow
2. Seven, sad, warm
3. bald, flat
4. huge, delicious
5. Two, brave, fat

Bottom
1. lazy, fat
2. hungry, birthday
3. Three, good
4. five, twelve
5. first

Page 283

Top
1. indoors
2. away
3. Here, there
4. outdoors
5. here

Bottom
1. around, around
2. Here
3. up, down
4. upstairs
5. up

Page 284

Top
1. tonight
2. Yesterday
3. always
4. when
5. sometime

Bottom
1. never
2. Then
3. tomorrow
4. now
5. yesterday

Page 285

Top
1. gladly
2. Slowly
3. carefully
4. silently
5. hard

Bottom
1. happily
2. Quickly
3. still
4. loudly
5. suddenly

Page 286

Top
1. Then, away
2. never, loudly
3. upstairs, downstairs
4. nearby
5. yesterday

Bottom
1. ever
2. outdoors
3. silently, upstairs
4. when
5. Sometimes, sometimes

Add the numbers and write the **sum**.

36 + 2	41 + 7	24 +12	30 + 8	52 + 7	34 + 5
9 +70	26 + 2	15 +11	23 + 6	18 + 1	6 +23
54 + 4	1 +18	22 +22	3 +16	48 + 0	14 +14

Draw a line from each problem to the correct answer.

6 + 6	22
11 + 11	18
7 + 9	14
8 + 10	12
8 + 6	16

9 + 8	23
12 + 9	18
7 + 11	17
11 + 12	21
12 + 0	12

Add the numbers and write the **sum**.

13 +24	51 + 8	30 +19	13 +63	20 +59	47 +21
7 +21	25 +22	11 +68	46 +31	30 +50	62 +26
32 +45	40 +40	35 +51	32 +32	43 +50	35 +34

Check it out.
One answer is wrong. Circle the **wrong** answer.

12 +12 24	11 + 2 13	13 + 6 19	5 +12 17
8 + 6 14	9 + 8 19	23 +12 35	7 +31 38

Read the problem. Write the numbers.
Add the numbers and write the **sum**.

Justin heard 37 loud harps. Justin heard 12 quiet harps. How many harps did Justin hear in all?

$$\begin{array}{r} 37 \\ +\ 12 \\ \hline 49 \end{array}$$

There were 15 big drums in the band. And there were 20 little drums. How many drums were there in all?

$$\begin{array}{r} \\ +\ \\ \hline \end{array}$$

Round School has 30 girl singers and 20 boy singers. How many singers does Round School have in all?

$$\begin{array}{r} \\ +\ \\ \hline \end{array}$$

Mr. Cash sold 24 old banjos and 24 new banjos. How many banjos did Mr. Cash sell in all?

$$\begin{array}{r} \\ +\ \\ \hline \end{array}$$

Lisa bought 2 music books at The Record Shop. She bought 3 music books at the school sale. And then she bought 4 music books at Ben's Barn. How many music books did Lisa buy?

Jon sold 4 drums to Round School. Then he sold 1 drum to Lisa. Last of all, he sold 2 drums to a tall drummer. How many drums did Jon sell in all?

Add the cents and write the **sum.**

10¢ + 8¢ ___¢	17¢ +11¢ ___¢	12¢ +12¢ ___¢	42¢ + 7¢ ___¢	23¢ +10¢ ___¢	20¢ +25¢ ___¢
5¢ +13¢ ___¢	18¢ + 1¢ ___¢	44¢ +44¢ ___¢	3¢ +74¢ ___¢	53¢ +16¢ ___¢	4¢ +51¢ ___¢
55¢ +10¢ ___¢	2¢ +45¢ ___¢	31¢ + 6¢ ___¢	11¢ +61¢ ___¢	64¢ +14¢ ___¢	38¢ +21¢ ___¢

Check it out.
Two answers are wrong. Circle the **wrong** answers.

3¢ + 3¢ 6¢	10¢ +10¢ 20¢	8¢ +11¢ 17¢	18¢ +20¢ 38¢
15¢ + 4¢ 19¢	25¢ + 0¢ 25¢	22¢ +25¢ 57¢	11¢ +43¢ 54¢

292

Add the numbers and write the **sum**.

45 +37 82	29 +34 63	45 +38	24 +66	71 +22	30 +60
14 +67	69 +26	54 +23	21 +78	79 +16	80 +14
43 +33	36 +25	48 +27	12 +77	73 +19	13 +72

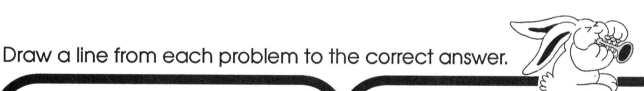

Draw a line from each problem to the correct answer.

20 + 20	50
10 + 25	45
20 + 30	50
35 + 10	40
25 + 25	35

9 + 20	31
10 + 21	41
9 + 21	29
11 + 30	81
40 + 41	30

Add the numbers and write the **sum**.

4	0	6	10	11	17
2	5	12	2	34	0
+ 2	+ 3	+ 1	+ 13	+ 4	+ 2

11	12	35	42	30	75
2	23	10	36	30	10
+ 13	+ 4	+ 13	+ 0	+ 30	+ 12

Draw a line from each problem to the correct answer.

20 + 50	70
40 + 20	90
60 + 20	40
20 + 20	80
30 + 60	60

22 + 22	88
33 + 33	48
44 + 44	44
41 + 41	82
24 + 24	66

294

Read the problem. Write the numbers.
Add the numbers and write the **sum**.

Wesley carried 22 large tubas. He also carried 14 small tubas. How many tubas did Wesley carry in all?

$+$ _____
_____

Kelly had 41 blue flutes and 9 yellow flutes. How many flutes did she have in all?

$+$ _____
_____

The piano player hit 76 sharp notes. She also hit 22 flat notes. How many notes did she hit in all?

$+$ _____
_____

On Monday I saw 53 trumpets. On Tuesday I saw 39 more trumpets. How many trumpets did I see in all?

$+$ _____
_____

I took 4 tubas to the band room. I rested. I took 2 more tubas to the band room. I ate a hamburger. I took the last 2 tubas to the band room. How many tubas did I take to the band room in all?

The dog chewed up 2 flutes. The cat chewed up 3 flutes. The mice chewed up 2 flutes. How many flutes did the animals chew up?

Add the numbers and write the **sum**.

123 + 51 174	47 +111	244 + 15	81 +300	97 +402	230 + 50
91 +108	202 + 85	100 + 61	265 + 24	82 +114	400 +225
131 + 31	62 +313	49 +350	83 +101	55 +104	248 + 41

Draw a line from each problem to the correct answer.

5 + 15	20
25 + 20	65
20 + 15	45
15 + 10	25
35 + 30	35

100 + 10	100
20 + 200	220
50 + 50	110
300 + 60	320
300 + 20	360

Add the dollars and cents.

$1.10 + .25 **$1.35**	$2.12 + .50 $.	$1.29 + .30 $.	$ .88 + 4.11 $.	$2.54 + .22 $.
$ .98 + 3.01 $.	$2.75 + .21 $.	$ .58 + 1.00 $.	$1.50 + .25 $.	$ .25 + 3.70 $.
$ .25 + 2.50 $.	$2.85 + .10 $.	$3.42 + .45 $.	$5.15 + .73 $.	$ .92 + 1.02 $.

Check it out.
One answer is wrong. Circle the **wrong** answer.

$2.00 + .50 $2.50	$3.00 + 6.00 $9.00	$ .62 + 3.10 $3.72	$4.40 + 3.30 $7.70
$1.50 + 1.40 $2.90	$ .75 + 2.10 $2.85	$1.30 + .55 $1.85	$1.42 + .53 $2.95

Add the numbers and write the **sum.**

92 +166 *258*	83 +208 *291*	360 + 99	84 +333	140 + 78	318 + 18
90 +185	86 +151	217 + 76	87 +407	299 + 80	94 +174
260 + 89	63 +118	325 +145	96 +122	103 +126	128 +304

Draw a line from each problem to the correct answer.

25 + 120	215
25 + 100	145
100 + 225	260
100 + 115	325
130 + 130	125

80 + 80	340
120 + 120	400
200 + 200	160
220 + 220	240
300 + 40	440

Add the numbers and write the **sum**.

100 +300	135 +254	322 +177	263 +115	280 +310	532 +142
102 +105	204 +211	312 +106	155 +340	302 +302	117 +260
520 +455	450 +420	107 +201	320 +109	112 +412	120 +120

Check it out.
Three answers are wrong. Circle the **wrong** answers.

200 +350 555	450 +220 670	601 +108 709	611 +116 727
543 +345 888	404 +222 606	123 +321 444	115 +213 327

Read the problem. Write the numbers.
Add the numbers and write the **sum**.

The scout had 100 bugles. The cook had 147 bugles. How many bugles did they have in all?

_____
+ _____
_____

Clint hit the gong 245 times. Then he hit it 344 times. How many times did Clint hit the gong in all?

_____
+ _____
_____

Dana counted 275 music sticks. Mike counted 210 more sticks. How many sticks did they count in all?

_____
+ _____
_____

The ape dropped 113 big drums off the cliff. Then he dropped 111 small drums off the cliff. How many drums did the ape drop in all?

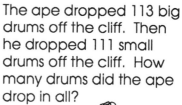

_____
+ _____
_____

The ape kicked the gong 120 times. The ape took a nap. The ape woke up and saw the gong. The ape kicked the gong 210 more times. How many times did the ape kick the gong in all?

Dana painted 80 music sticks red. Wow! She loved the way they looked. She painted 205 music sticks yellow. How many sticks did she paint?

Add the numbers and write the **sum**.

$$\begin{array}{r} 14 \\ 10 \\ +8 \\ \hline 32 \end{array} \qquad \begin{array}{r} 50 \\ 50 \\ +50 \\ \hline 150 \end{array} \qquad \begin{array}{r} 45 \\ 31 \\ +31 \\ \hline \end{array} \qquad \begin{array}{r} 12 \\ 40 \\ +7 \\ \hline \end{array} \qquad \begin{array}{r} 53 \\ 43 \\ +23 \\ \hline \end{array} \qquad \begin{array}{r} 14 \\ 2 \\ +17 \\ \hline \end{array}$$

$$\begin{array}{r} 26 \\ 11 \\ +15 \\ \hline \end{array} \qquad \begin{array}{r} 48 \\ 12 \\ +8 \\ \hline \end{array} \qquad \begin{array}{r} 19 \\ 18 \\ +22 \\ \hline \end{array} \qquad \begin{array}{r} 10 \\ 15 \\ +27 \\ \hline \end{array} \qquad \begin{array}{r} 30 \\ 20 \\ +50 \\ \hline \end{array} \qquad \begin{array}{r} 9 \\ 30 \\ +55 \\ \hline \end{array}$$

Draw a line from each problem to the correct answer.

230 + 130	290	400 + 50	550
240 + 140	380	500 + 50	300
110 + 180	360	50 + 300	350
190 + 300	490	50 + 250	500
280 + 100	380	450 + 50	450

Add the dollars and cents.

$$\begin{array}{r}\overset{1}{\$}1.20 \\ + \ .88 \\ \hline \$2.08\end{array}$$

$$\begin{array}{r}\$ \ .14 \\ + \ 2.71 \\ \hline \$ \ .\end{array}$$

$$\begin{array}{r}\$3.63 \\ + \ .36 \\ \hline \$ \ .\end{array}$$

$$\begin{array}{r}\$2.00 \\ + \ .02 \\ \hline \$ \ .\end{array}$$

$$\begin{array}{r}\$1.80 \\ + \ .80 \\ \hline \$ \ .\end{array}$$

$$\begin{array}{r}\$2.15 \\ + \ .25 \\ \hline \$ \ .\end{array}$$

$$\begin{array}{r}\$1.88 \\ + \ .07 \\ \hline \$ \ .\end{array}$$

$$\begin{array}{r}\$ \ .15 \\ + \ 3.75 \\ \hline \$ \ .\end{array}$$

$$\begin{array}{r}\$4.10 \\ + \ .95 \\ \hline \$ \ .\end{array}$$

$$\begin{array}{r}\$ \ .17 \\ + \ 1.67 \\ \hline \$ \ .\end{array}$$

$$\begin{array}{r}\$ \ .50 \\ + \ 4.65 \\ \hline \$ \ .\end{array}$$

$$\begin{array}{r}\$1.17 \\ + \ .99 \\ \hline \$ \ .\end{array}$$

$$\begin{array}{r}\$ \ .24 \\ + \ 1.38 \\ \hline \$ \ .\end{array}$$

$$\begin{array}{r}\$1.91 \\ + \ .56 \\ \hline \$ \ .\end{array}$$

$$\begin{array}{r}\$2.57 \\ + \ .38 \\ \hline \$ \ .\end{array}$$

Check it out.
Two answers are wrong. Circle the **wrong** answers.

$$\begin{array}{r}\$ \ .20 \\ + \ 1.50 \\ \hline \$1.70\end{array}$$

$$\begin{array}{r}\$8.32 \\ + \ .50 \\ \hline \$8.82\end{array}$$

$$\begin{array}{r}\$6.15 \\ + \ .91 \\ \hline \$7.06\end{array}$$

$$\begin{array}{r}\$ \ .50 \\ + \ 1.50 \\ \hline \$2.00\end{array}$$

$$\begin{array}{r}\$9.00 \\ + \ .35 \\ \hline \$9.35\end{array}$$

$$\begin{array}{r}\$1.92 \\ + \ .56 \\ \hline \$1.48\end{array}$$

$$\begin{array}{r}\$1.20 \\ + \ .88 \\ \hline \$3.08\end{array}$$

$$\begin{array}{r}\$4.17 \\ + \ .17 \\ \hline \$4.34\end{array}$$

Add the numbers and write the **sum**.

480 +146 *626*	124 +239 *363*	367 +366	128 +435	171 +188	269 +306
592 +209	125 +125	194 +510	221 +169	368 +232	444 +266
365 +264	243 +267	362 +378	179 +161	163 +277	380 +160

Draw a line from each problem to the correct answer.

500 + 400	800
400 + 300	810
200 + 600	700
800 + 10	600
100 + 500	900

111 + 111	333
222 + 222	444
222 + 111	222
333 + 333	444
111 + 333	666

Subtract the numbers and write the **difference**.

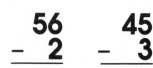

$$
\begin{array}{cccccc}
56 & 45 & 98 & 87 & 40 & 34 \\
-\ 2 & -\ 3 & -15 & -\ 6 & -20 & -\ 1 \\
\end{array}
$$

$$
\begin{array}{cccccc}
92 & 30 & 89 & 73 & 17 & 48 \\
-\ 2 & -10 & -\ 7 & -\ 3 & -\ 5 & -28 \\
\end{array}
$$

$$
\begin{array}{cccccc}
66 & 18 & 59 & 99 & 57 & 70 \\
-13 & -\ 5 & -29 & -\ 2 & -\ 3 & -50 \\
\end{array}
$$

Draw a line from each problem to the correct answer.

12 – 2	7
10 – 4	10
8 – 1	1
10 – 9	4
6 – 2	6

8 – 8	8
10 – 3	3
8 – 0	7
12 – 3	0
11 – 8	9

304

Subtract the numbers and write the **difference**.

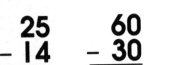

25 – 14	60 – 30	27 – 16	79 – 19	84 – 43	22 – 10
76 – 35	63 – 42	98 – 75	51 – 31	70 – 60	49 – 28
88 – 67	90 – 50	23 – 12	58 – 37	44 – 33	65 – 32

Check it out.
One answer is wrong. Circle the **wrong** answer.

87 – 21 66	39 – 16 23	60 – 50 10	57 – 22 34
18 – 2 16	51 – 11 40	82 – 50 32	64 – 52 12

Subtract the cents.

68¢	54¢	46¢	39¢	47¢	50¢
− 10¢	− 21¢	− 13¢	− 15¢	− 26¢	− 10¢
___¢	___¢	___¢	___¢	___¢	___¢

69¢	77¢	38¢	82¢	26¢	64¢
− 39¢	− 5¢	− 24¢	− 52¢	− 26¢	− 41¢
___¢	___¢	___¢	___¢	___¢	___¢

78¢	18¢	97¢	86¢	68¢	94¢
− 53¢	− 7¢	− 36¢	− 62¢	− 34¢	− 93¢
___¢	___¢	___¢	___¢	___¢	___¢

Check it out.
Two answers are wrong. Circle the **wrong** answers.

65¢	64¢	99¢	86¢
− 22¢	− 10¢	− 50¢	− 83¢
43¢	50¢	49¢	3¢

36¢	54¢	95¢	27¢
− 25¢	− 54¢	− 10¢	− 12¢
1¢	0¢	85¢	15¢

Read the problem. Write the numbers.
Subtract the numbers and write the **difference**.

Petra Piper had 81 pipes.
She gave away 40 pipes.
How many pipes did
she have left?

81
− 40
41

There were 85 singers
at Round School. Then
33 singers went away.
How many singers
were left?

——————
— ——————

——————

The captain of the band
saw 77 tubas. She broke
22 of the tubas. How
many tubas were left?

——————
— ——————

——————

Eric had 56 flutes.
He sold 14 flutes.
How many flutes did
he have left?

——————
— ——————

——————

Kara counted 32 singers. But
Peter counted 88 singers.
How many more singers did
Peter count?

The ape found 57 guitar
strings. The ape lost 34 of
the strings. How many
guitar strings did the ape
have left?

Subtract the numbers and write the **difference**.

80 − 31 **49**	91 − 46 **45**	25 − 16	83 − 49	36 − 27	74 − 18
57 − 42	72 − 58	90 − 74	40 − 33	68 − 49	21 − 18
72 − 66	30 − 15	71 − 69	79 − 60	43 − 25	65 − 49

Draw a line from each problem to the correct answer.

70 − 20	40		80 − 60	25
90 − 20	15		50 − 25	55
85 − 45	70		75 − 50	30
35 − 25	50		65 − 10	20
25 − 10	10		70 − 40	25

Subtract the numbers and write the **difference**.

197	141	248	189	326	255
− 26	− 30	− 35	− 67	− 26	− 11
171					

154	173	222	279	134	219
− 43	− 42	− 12	− 49	− 13	− 18

358	124	487	290	395	346
− 45	− 10	−487	− 70	− 52	− 15

Check it out.
Three answers are wrong. Circle the **wrong** answers.

118	234	89	395
− 15	−123	− 27	− 11
113	111	62	394

178	27	874	184
− 53	− 6	− 270	− 103
125	21	600	81

Read the problem. Write the numbers.
Subtract the numbers and write the **difference**.

There were 180 bands in the marching band contest. Then 70 bands went home. How many bands were left?

———
—
———

Haley had 117 records. She broke 16 of them. How many records did Haley have left?

———
—
———

Peter counted 259 notes in one song. He counted 33 notes in another song. How many more notes were in the first song?

———
—
———

There were 298 radios in Round School. There were 86 radios in Baxter School. How many more radios were in Round School?

———
—
———

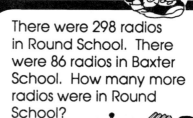

Baxter School singers won 147 blue ribbons. Round School singers won 112 blue ribbons. How many more ribbons did the Baxter School singers win?

The ape ate 235 dusty old records and 100 clean new records. How many more dusty old records than clean records did the ape eat?

310

Subtract the dollars and cents.

$1.49	$2.88	$3.54	$2.12	$1.27
− .37	− .85	− .11	− .12	− .06
$1.12	$.	$.	$.	$.

$1.86	$3.11	$2.93	$4.65	$1.60
− .53	− .00	− .22	− .54	− .30
$.	$.	$.	$.	$.

$2.58	$3.79	$3.57	$4.99	$4.24
− .46	− .58	− .15	− .65	− .10
$.	$.	$.	$.	$.

Check it out.
Two answers are wrong. Circle the **wrong** answers.

$5.73	$4.53	$3.27	$8.52
− .72	− .12	− .20	− .30
$5.01	$4.31	$3.07	$8.22

$6.45	$1.68	$9.99	$2.71
− .33	− .53	− .87	− .30
$6.12	$1.15	$9.22	$2.41

Subtract the numbers and write the **difference**.

187 −135 **52**	261 −200	478 −405	657 −332	416 −205	744 −622
199 −139	235 −121	390 −240	473 −132	789 −348	237 −137
679 −546	382 −251	437 −214	647 −603	741 −500	639 −327

Draw a line from each problem to the correct answer.

200 − 100	0
300 − 300	300
300 − 100	200
300 − 0	200
400 − 200	100

450 − 50	150
250 − 100	400
200 − 50	350
450 − 100	50
300 − 250	150

Subtract the numbers and write the **difference**.

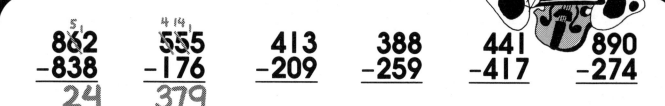

$$
\begin{array}{r} \overset{5}{8}62 \\ -838 \\ \hline 24 \end{array}
\qquad
\begin{array}{r} \overset{4}{5}\overset{14}{5}\overset{1}{5} \\ -176 \\ \hline 379 \end{array}
\qquad
\begin{array}{r} 413 \\ -209 \\ \hline \end{array}
\qquad
\begin{array}{r} 388 \\ -259 \\ \hline \end{array}
\qquad
\begin{array}{r} 441 \\ -417 \\ \hline \end{array}
\qquad
\begin{array}{r} 890 \\ -274 \\ \hline \end{array}
$$

$$
\begin{array}{r} 377 \\ -158 \\ \hline \end{array}
\qquad
\begin{array}{r} 719 \\ -476 \\ \hline \end{array}
\qquad
\begin{array}{r} 193 \\ -148 \\ \hline \end{array}
\qquad
\begin{array}{r} 321 \\ -192 \\ \hline \end{array}
\qquad
\begin{array}{r} 954 \\ -788 \\ \hline \end{array}
\qquad
\begin{array}{r} 739 \\ -665 \\ \hline \end{array}
$$

$$
\begin{array}{r} 336 \\ -190 \\ \hline \end{array}
\qquad
\begin{array}{r} 328 \\ -143 \\ \hline \end{array}
\qquad
\begin{array}{r} 315 \\ -291 \\ \hline \end{array}
\qquad
\begin{array}{r} 716 \\ -648 \\ \hline \end{array}
\qquad
\begin{array}{r} 800 \\ -711 \\ \hline \end{array}
\qquad
\begin{array}{r} 673 \\ -567 \\ \hline \end{array}
$$

Draw a line from each problem to the correct answer.

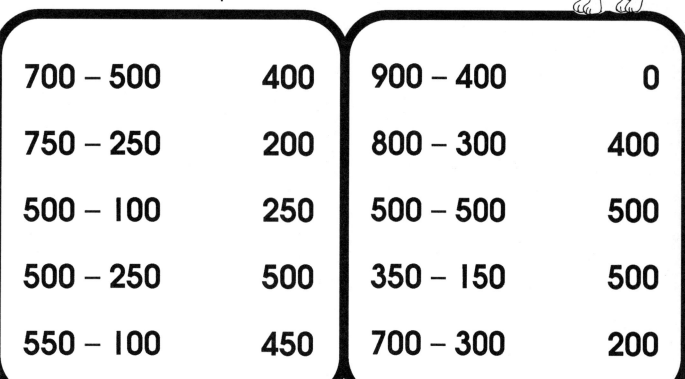

700 – 500	400
750 – 250	200
500 – 100	250
500 – 250	500
550 – 100	450

900 – 400	0
800 – 300	400
500 – 500	500
350 – 150	500
700 – 300	200

Read the problem. Write the numbers.
Subtract the numbers and write the **difference**.

Craig fixed 324 record players. Brenda fixed 249. How many more record players did Craig fix.

_____
_
_____

Patrick sang 187 songs. Danny sang 159 songs. How many more songs did Patrick sing?

_____
_
_____

Gretchen rolled 536 drums down the road. Kevin rolled 428 drums. How many more drums did Gretchen roll?

_____
_
_____

Kerry counted 600 trombones in the parade. Terry counted 385 trombones. How many more trombones did Kerry count?

_____
_
_____

Jeff saw 800 drummers in the parade. Lora saw 450 drummers. How many more drummers did Jeff see?

Kyle sang "Row, Row, Row" 225 times. Mike sang "Row, Row, Row" only 120 times. How many more times did Kyle sing the song than Mike?

314

Subtract the numbers and write the **difference**.

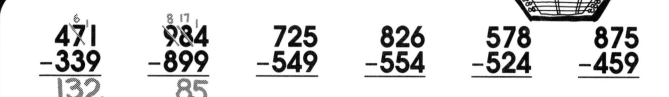

471	984	725	826	578	875
−339	−899	−549	−554	−524	−459
132	85				

999	652	593	947	670	929
−779	−447	−376	−657	−590	−851

746	811	925	714	635	700
−462	−773	−850	−576	−481	−458

Draw a line from each problem to the correct answer.

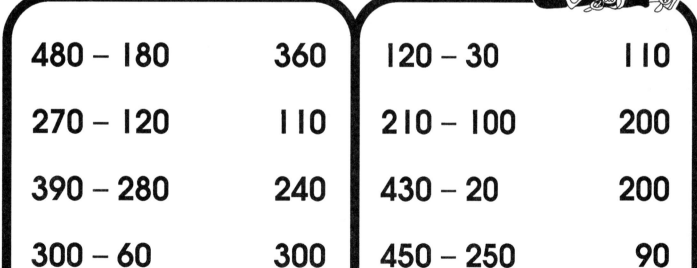

480 − 180	360
270 − 120	110
390 − 280	240
300 − 60	300
400 − 40	150

120 − 30	110
210 − 100	200
430 − 20	200
450 − 250	90
700 − 500	410

Subtract the dollars and cents.

$6.15 − 4.00 $.	$2.86 − 2.29 $.	$7.65 − 6.89 $.	$3.38 − 1.52 $.	$1.96 − 1.78 $.
$9.61 − 7.57 $.	$3.94 − 2.68 $.	$7.95 − 5.85 $.	$8.08 − 7.21 $.	$2.82 − 1.53 $.
$5.27 − 4.57 $.	$7.50 − 3.75 $.	$6.88 − 5.88 $.	$4.52 − 3.09 $.	$6.08 − .99 $.

Check it out.
One answer is wrong. Circle the **wrong** answer.

$5.79 − .65 $5.14	$6.19 − 5.08 $1.11	$8.22 − 1.11 $7.11	$4.50 − .50 $4.00
$5.52 − 2.21 $2.31	$5.16 − 1.14 $4.02	$2.37 − 1.20 $1.17	$6.24 − 5.12 $1.12

Do you **add** or **subtract** to solve the problem?
Write the numbers and solve the problem.

Round School bought 233 harps. Baxter School bought 184 harps. How many more harps did Round School buy?

_____

□ _____

_____

Lindsay sang for 355 days. Matthew sang for 314 days. How many more days did Lindsay sing?

_____

□ _____

_____

Baxter School bought 242 drums and Round School bought 276 drums. How many drums did they buy in all?

_____

□ _____

_____

Jack's band gave 373 concerts. Jennifer's band gave 253 concerts. How many concerts did the bands give in all?

_____

□ _____

_____

Jack's band gave 373 concerts. Jennifer's band gave 253 concerts. How many more concerts did Jack's band give?

Lindsay sang 35 new songs. Carl also sang 35 new songs. How many songs did they sing in all?

Do you **add** or **subtract** to solve the problem?
Write the numbers and solve the problem.

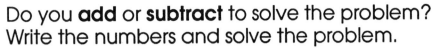

One year Mitchell wrote 359 songs. The next year he wrote 247 songs. How many songs did he write in all?

□ ____ ____
  ____

Karen sang 558 times in one year. The next year, she sang 449 times. How many more times did she sing the first year?

□ ____ ____
  ____

Round School sold 513 tickets to Band Day. Baxter School sold 466 tickets to Band Day. How many tickets did the schools sell in all?

□ ____ ____
  ____

The train carried 273 organs. But 165 organs fell off the train. How many organs were left?

□ ____ ____
  ____

Darla drew 999 musical notes. But her sister erased 332 of them. How many notes did Darla have left?

You know that Mitchell wrote 359 songs one year. You know he wrote 247 songs the next year. How many songs did he write in all?

318

Page 289
Top
38,48,36,38,59,39
79,28,26,29,19,29
58,19,44,19,48,28

Bottom
12	17
22	21
16	18
18	23
14	12

Page 290
Top
37,59,49,76,79,68
28,47,79,77,80,88
77,80,86,64,93,69

Bottom
9 + 8 ≠ 19

Page 291
Top
49,35
50,48

Bottom
9,7

Page 292
Top
18¢,28¢,24¢,49¢,33¢,45¢
18¢,19¢,88¢,77¢,69¢,55¢
65¢,47¢,37¢,72¢,78¢,59¢

Bottom
8¢ + 11¢ ≠ 17¢
22¢ + 25¢ ≠ 57¢

Page 293
Top
82,63,83,90,93,90
81,95,77,99,95,94
76,61,75,89,92,85

Bottom
40	29
35	31
50	30
45	41
50	81

Page 294
Top
8,8,19,25,49,19
26,39,58,78,90,97

Bottom
70	44
60	66
80	88
40	82
90	48

Page 295
Top
36,50
98,92

Bottom
8,7

Page 296
Top
174,158,259,381,499,280
199,287,161,289,196,625
162,375,399,184,159,289

Bottom
20	110
45	220
35	100
25	360
65	320

Page 297
Top
$1.35, $2.62, $1.59, $4.99, $2.76
$3.99, $2.96, $1.58, $1.75, $3.95
$2.75, $2.95, $3.87, $5.88, $1.94

Bottom
$1.42 + .53 = $2.95

Page 298
Top
258,291,459,417,218,336
275,237,293,494,379,268
349,181,470,218,229,432

Bottom
145	160
125	240
325	400
215	440
260	340

Page 299
Top
400,389,499,378,590,674
207,415,418,495,604,377
975,870,308,429,524,240

Bottom
200 + 350 ≠ 555
404 + 222 ≠ 606
115 + 213 ≠ 327

Page 300
Top
247,589
485,224

Bottom
330,285

Page 301
Top
32,150,107,59,119,33
52,68,59,52,100,94

Bottom
360	450
380	550
290	350
490	300
380	500

Page 302
Top
$2.08, $2.85, $3.99, $2.02, $2.60
$2.40, $1.95, $3.90, $5.05, $1.84
$5.15, $2.16, $1.62, $2.47, $2.95

Bottom
$1.92 + .56 ≠ $1.48
$1.20 + .88 ≠ $3.08

Page 303

Top
626, 363, 733, 563, 359, 575
801, 250, 704, 390, 600, 710
629, 510, 740, 340, 440, 540

Bottom

900	222
700	444
800	333
810	666
600	444

Page 304

Top
54, 42, 83, 81, 20, 33
90, 20, 82, 70, 12, 20
53, 13, 30, 97, 54, 20

Bottom

10	0
6	7
7	8
1	9
4	3

Page 305

Top
11, 30, 11, 60, 41, 12
41, 21, 23, 20, 10, 21
21, 40, 11, 21, 11, 33

Bottom
57 − 22 ≠ 34

Page 306

Top
58¢, 33¢, 33¢, 24¢, 21¢, 40¢
30¢, 72¢, 14¢, 30¢, 0¢, 23¢
25¢, 11¢, 61¢, 24¢, 34¢, 1¢

Bottom
64¢ − 10¢ ≠ 50¢
36¢ − 25¢ ≠ 1¢

Page 307

Top
41, 52
55, 42

Bottom
56, 23

Page 308

Top
49, 45, 9, 34, 9, 56
15, 14, 16, 7, 19, 3
6, 15, 2, 19, 18, 16

Bottom

50	20
70	25
40	25
10	55
15	30

Page 309

Top
171, 111, 213, 122, 300, 244
111, 131, 210, 230, 121, 201
313, 114, 0, 220, 343, 331

Bottom
118 − 15 ≠ 113
395 − 11 ≠ 394
874 − 270 ≠ 600

Page 310

Top
110, 101
226, 212

Bottom
35, 135

Page 311

Top
$1.12, $2.03, $3.43, $2.00, $1.21
$1.33, $3.11, $2.71, $4.11, $1.30
$2.12, $3.21, $3.42, $4.34, $4.14

Bottom
$4.53 − .12 ≠ $4.31
$9.99 − .87 ≠ $9.22

Page 312

Top
52, 61, 73, 325, 211, 122
60, 114, 150, 341, 441, 100
133, 131, 223, 44, 241, 312

Bottom

100	400
0	150
200	150
300	350
200	50

Page 313

Top
24, 379, 204, 129, 24, 616
219, 243, 45, 129, 166, 74
146, 185, 24, 68, 89, 106

Bottom

200	500
500	500
400	0
250	200
450	400

Page 314

Top
75, 28
108, 215

Bottom
350, 105

Page 315

Top
132, 85, 176, 272, 54, 416
220, 205, 217, 290, 80, 78
284, 38, 75, 138, 154, 242

Bottom

300	90
150	110
110	410
240	200
360	200

Page 316

Top
$2.15, $.57, $.76, $1.86, $.18
$2.04, $1.26, $2.10, $.87, $1.29
$.70, $3.75, $1.00, $1.43, $5.09

Bottom
$5.52 − $2.21 ≠ $2.31

Page 317

Top
49, 41
518, 626

Bottom
120, 70

Page 318

Top
606, 109
979, 108

Bottom
667, 606